THE JOBLESS LAWYER'S HANDBOOK

How to Get Hired as a Lawyer

Brian H. Potts

Copyright © 2021 Brian H. Potts
All rights reserved. No part of this publication may be reproduced, distributed, or transmitted in any form or by any means, including photocopying, recording, or other electronic or mechanical methods, without the prior written permission of the author, except in the case of brief quotations embodied in critical reviews and certain other noncommercial uses permitted by copyright law.
For permission requests, contact the publisher at:

www.Holon.co

ISBN#: 978-1-955342-30-8 (Hardback)
ISBN#: 978-1-955342-20-9 (Paperback)
ISBN#: 978-1-955342-34-6 (eBook)

Published by:

Holon Publishing & Collective Press
A Storytelling Company
www.Holon.co

This book is dedicated to the tens of thousands of jobless lawyers and law students out there.

You can do it.

Contents

Introduction	1
Chapter 1: Law Jobs Are Not Like Regular Jobs	5
Chapter 2: Get Your Shit Together	8
Chapter 3: Figure Out Where You Stand in the Job Market	13
Chapter 4: What They Don't Tell You in Law School	18
Chapter 5: Geography Matters	27
Chapter 6: Network, Network, Network	32
Chapter 7: How to Get People to Meet with You	39
Chapter 8: Spam, Spam, Spam	47
Chapter 9: The Cold Email	52
Chapter 10: How to Perfect Your Resume	57
Chapter 11: Your Writing Sample and Cover Letter Aren't that Good	65
Chapter 12: How to Find Job Postings Online	75
Chapter 13: Things NOT to Do When Hunting for a Job	80
Chapter 14: Six People Interrogating You (A.K.A. the Interview)	85
Chapter 15: What to Do When You Finally Land a Job	95
Chapter 16: Jumping Ship	97
Chapter 17: Understanding the Business of Law	101
Chapter 18: To Specialize or Not to Specialize	107
Chapter 19: Advice for Foreign-Trained Lawyers	110
Chapter 20: The LL.M Conundrum	117
Chapter 21: How to Succeed as a Lawyer	123
Your Get-a-Job Checklist	127

Introduction

Hello! *Welcome to The Jobless Lawyer's Handbook.* By starting this book, you've taken a step in the right direction towards landing your dream job. Soon you'll be sitting in an office somewhere, chained to your desk, spending nine or ten hours a day doing legal work.

It's going to be great!

Although it's a handbook, I recommend you read this book from cover to cover. In fact, I recommend you do so as soon as possible.

I wrote this book for 1Ls, 2Ls, 3Ls, LL.Ms, and recent graduates who aren't in their dream jobs. It's packed with a lot of useful information. And to save you time, I've labeled sections you can skip based on your seniority as a lawyer and job status.

Before we begin, however, let me give you a little background about me.

When I was in law school, I applied to work at every top 100 law firm in the U.S.—and I got form rejection letters from all of them. All 100 firms sent me a two-sentence "No thank you" letter via the U.S. mail. None of them even interviewed me.

Going to my mailbox everyday only to find it full of rejection letters was hell. It caused me to go through four of the five stages of grief. Denial first. Then anger. Followed by depression. Finally, acceptance.

I had to accept being rejected. What else could I do? I wasn't going to call them up and beg.

Instead, I used those rejection letters as motivation. I kept all of them. I then set out to prove that every one of those white-shoe law firms was wrong about me.

And I did.

I ended up being the youngest in my partner class at one of

those top-ranked law firms. Today I'm an equity partner and the co-chair of a practice group at another.

I scraped my way to the top. To get there, I used a lot of the methods in this book.

Be forewarned: this book is blunt. Some might call it crass. That's intentional. You might not agree with some of my recommendations and aggressive approaches. That's fine. Everyone needs to find their own path.

But hopefully you'll come away from this book having landed your dream job. That's my goal. It should be yours too. If I'm a little over the top, please remember that my intentions are good. (And I'm trying to keep your attention.)

One random day many years later, I was digging through a box in my garage, and I found those rejection letters. All 100 of them, including the one from my current law firm, Perkins Coie.

I'm kind of a silly and sarcastic fellow. So, I decided to frame my Perkins Coie rejection letter, hang it on my office wall, and post a picture of it on LinkedIn.

The caption read: "Law students: if at first you don't succeed, try try again."

The post went viral; four and a half million people saw it. And I was quickly inundated with requests from law students and recent grads wanting to meet me via video to hear my story.

I met with all of them. One at a time. It started out as a way to give back during the pandemic. But now I'm hooked.

I set aside an hour in my calendar every day to help young lawyers and law students. When I meet with them, I hear their stories, give them advice, and refer them to other mentors. I actively try to address their concerns and answer their questions.

I've met with and mentored nearly three hundred law students and lawyers on the job hunt. I find myself recommending a lot of the same stuff.

My wife had the brilliant idea to write it all down, so I did,

Brian H. Potts · 1st
Partner at Perkins Coie - Forbes Contributor - Entrepreneur - Professor ...
1yr

Law students: if at first you don't succeed, try try again.

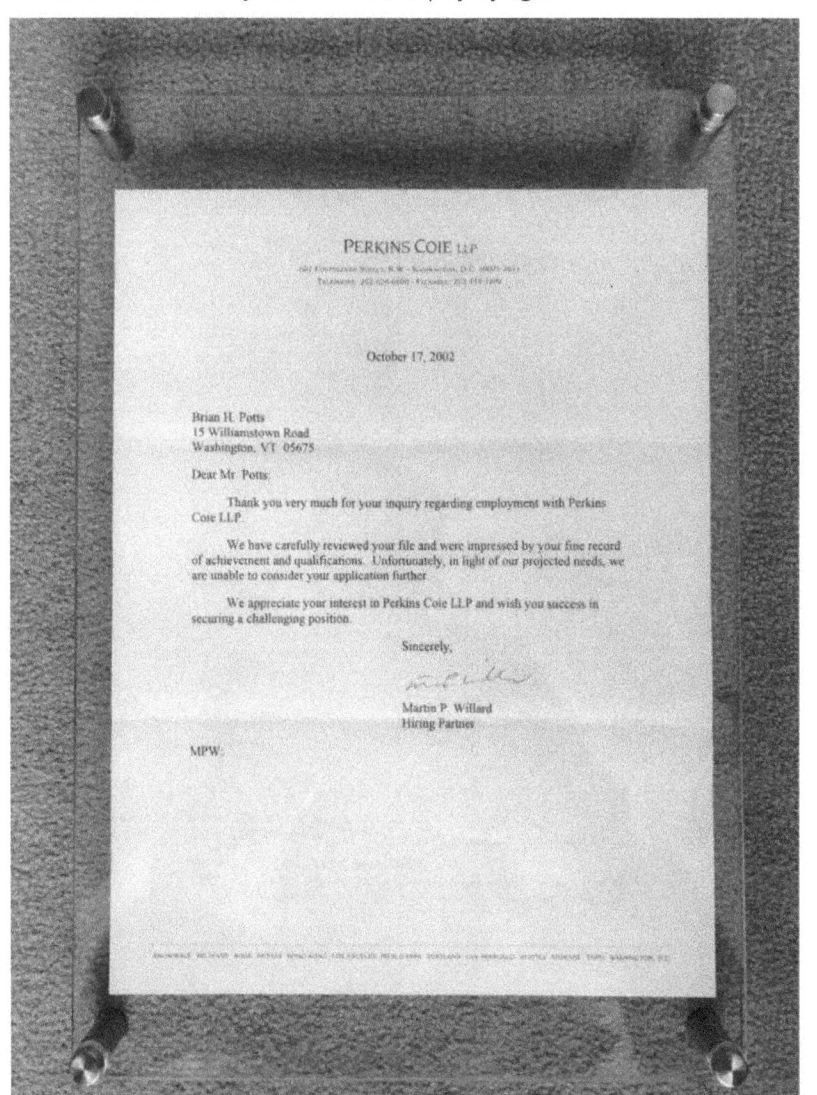

PERKINS COIE LLP

October 17, 2002

Brian H. Potts
15 Williamstown Road
Washington, VT 05675

Dear Mr. Potts:

Thank you very much for your inquiry regarding employment with Perkins Coie LLP.

We have carefully reviewed your file and were impressed by your fine record of achievement and qualifications. Unfortunately, in light of our projected needs, we are unable to consider your application further.

We appreciate your interest in Perkins Coie LLP and wish you success in securing a challenging position.

Sincerely,

Martin P. Willard
Hiring Partner

MPW

along with many of my mentees' stories. I hope their successes combined with the proven tools in this book will inspire you to keep at your job search.

And who knows?

Hopefully soon, you'll have a rejection letter of your own to hang on your office wall.

DISCLAIMER: I wrote this book. Me. Not my law firm. Not my clients. Not my mentees. Not anyone else I know or have ever encountered. As such, please don't blame them for my shenanigans.

CHAPTER 1:
Law Jobs Are Not Like Regular Jobs

Forget everything you've learned about getting a job. I don't care how many jobs you've had. Or how successful or unsuccessful you were in your prior profession.

Law jobs are not like regular jobs. You can't just drive around looking for "Help Wanted" signs. You can't just apply to the most interesting postings you find online.

Landing in your dream job is going to be difficult. According to the Bureau of Labor Statistics, 32,300 new lawyer jobs will be created over the next ten years. That might sound like a lot, but 35,000 law students graduate each year.

And it gets worse.

According to BLS and ABA statistics, there are only 819,000 employed lawyers out of a total of 1.35 million licensed lawyers in the U.S. today—which equates to 61%.

Here's the bottom line: for many of you, getting a legal job is going to be hard. Very hard. So, don't half-ass your attempt. Whether you graduate first in your class or second to last, you're going to have to put in work. Getting your dream job isn't going to be easy.

Get your priorities straight. In order of priority: getting a law job should beat out school, your side job, your bar studies, your friends, your binge TV, your video games, and maybe even your significant other.

The average person spends about 20,000 hours in school from kindergarten through graduating with a Juris Doctorate. If you take one thing away from this book, make sure it's this: You spend all of that time in school to prepare yourself so you can eventually get a job that you'll love—if you have to spend a few hundred hours trying to actually land that job, isn't that worth it?

<u>Absolutely.</u>

Being lazy or complacent isn't going to cut it. The more opportunities you create for yourself, the better your chances of success will be.

That's why you should be scouring every job website—all the time. You should know every federal and state agency hiring website by heart. You should be bookmarking every large-company-that-you-might-be-interested-in-working-for's "Open Positions" page. You should check all your bookmarked websites at least daily. Maybe even twice a day.

And the odds are pretty good that still won't be enough. That's where networking comes in.

Estimates vary, but there are more than a few studies that have found that 70-85% of people ended up in their current job thanks to networking. (If you don't believe me, Google it.)

So, even if you're the master of all the job listing websites and are applying everywhere, you're still not maximizing your potential opportunities.

You need to get to know as many people as you can. Starting now. You shouldn't stop until you find your dream job (or maybe even until you retire). <u>Never stop meeting and connecting with people.</u> That is the real ticket. The more people you interact with and get to know, the higher your chances are of landing your dream job.

I'll tell you how to network effectively, and without being smarmy, later. It's a skill you'll have to learn. This is true even if you're introverted (like me). And yes, it's true even if you think you're good at networking now. You can't be too good at networking.

Because selling is hard. Selling yourself is even harder. You can't be shy. Or worry about what people think. Not your colleagues. Not your classmates. Not your law professors. Not your placement office personnel. Not some random practicing attorney you spam. Not even your parents. This is about you and only you. This is about what you want. What you need. Where and what you get to do with your life.

Because if you sell yourself well, you'll get more opportunities. Which will give you more options. Which will ultimately increase your odds of landing your dream job.

Now, let's get to work.

CHAPTER 2:
Get Your Shit Together

I don't mean psychologically. I can't help you with that. I mean your schedule, your online profile, your looks, and your attitude.

One of your jobs now is to get a job.

If you don't get your shit together and set aside concrete times to work on figuring out ways to get other humans to hire you, you'll end up reading this book, vow to do some of the less-crazy stuff in here, do a few things, and then your efforts will fade. In three months, you'll be telling people my book sucked and didn't work.

I can't have that.

So please, for my sake, do the following.

Set aside time in your schedule for your job search.

You'll need to set aside time each day to work on your job search. Or at least you'll need to set aside an exact number of hours each week.

Be specific and rigid.

Put the job search times in your Outlook or other calendar for the next three months (at least). Then stick to your schedule. Treat each scheduled job search time as you would classes or any other professional time.

Now, how long should you spend working on getting a job? That's up to you.

If you're unemployed, the answer is easy: getting a job should be your full-time job. Treat it as such.

But, if you're in law school or studying for the bar exam, I'd shoot for spending an hour a day. Which might sound like a lot. Until you do the math: if you work on getting a job for an hour a day, five days a week, for fifty weeks—that's 250 total hours. That's a lot of time. But it's not unreasonable. I mean, hell, if you land a Biglaw associate position, they'll expect you to spend that much time doing non-billable, grunt marketing work for the firm every year.

You may as well start doing it now to market yourself.

But don't overwhelm yourself. Ease into it. If you're a 1L, maybe start out by setting aside 30 minutes a day so you don't burn yourself out. But then stick to it like an exercise or eating routine.

I'll say that again in case you didn't hear me the first time: *stick to it.*

Setting the schedule is the easy part. Sticking to it is what will start to separate you from the pack.

Clean up your online profile.

This should go without saying, but I'm going to say it anyway: people will Google you. They'll search for you on LinkedIn, YouTube, Facebook, Twitter, Pinterest, Instagram, Reddit, and Bumble. OK, maybe not Bumble.

They won't tell you that they internet stalked you. But they'll do it. They may even run credit checks on you.

So, figure out now what that means. And remedy any problems, if you can.

Start by Googling your name both with and without quotes. If I search for Brian Potts without quotes, I find a lot of stuff about other people. But if I put my name in quotes and search "Brian Potts," I still find other people's stuff; but not as much. If I search "Brian H. Potts" in quotes, I only find stuff about me.

Now do that for yourself. Go through at least four or five Google pages. See what comes up. Read anything about you. Look at the photos. Think about what a middle-aged lawyer mom with two kids who's not getting any sleep might think of your Google results. Or what a stuffy, corporate, grey-haired, pipe smoking, white-shoe partner might think.

Then do the same thing on all of your social media accounts. Delete posts that could be considered unprofessional.

Was it fun funneling beers last year at Daytona? Damn right it was. But those photos are not going to sit well with the law firm partners deciding whether to hire you (unless they're me).

Finally, once your accounts are as scrubbed as they can be, revise them to make them more professional.

Focus particularly on your LinkedIn profile. Make sure your profile has a professional picture. Make sure the "About Me" section is up to date. Make sure you've entered in every school or job you've worked at that might be relevant to lawyering. And, as always, make sure there are no typos (or emojis) in any of your online profiles.

If you aren't certain about your writing, have a few friends and family read your profiles. Yes, a few.

Clean yourself up.

I could go so many ways here with that heading.

But I'm going to start with the way you talk. (If you went to prep schools in New England, you can skip the next few paragraphs.)

I grew up in rural Kentucky. I had a lot of fun, and I did a lot of things I shouldn't have in high school. I grew up in college—but only a little.

Let's just say that my young life's purpose was to be a cautionary tale for others.

If I had a conversation with my senior-in-college-self now, I'd probably think I was unprofessional, meandering, and uneducated. I wouldn't even begin to take young me seriously. Not because of my slight Southern accent; because of my unprofessional air, over-the-top behavior, incessant cussing, and propensity to quote lines from the movie *Friday*.

I'm an adult now. And, as much as it pains me to say it, you have to clean up your language and start acting and talking like an adult if you want adults to hire you.

Your appearance matters too, of course. But I know my lanes. That's not one of them.

All I'll say is dress professionally. That doesn't mean wear a tie or skirt everywhere. It means comb your hair. Don't Zoom with people in your pajamas (at least on the top). Don't wear the same clothes you wore yesterday. You're a professional now, like it or not.

<u>And don't get drunk with anyone who might hire you.</u> Imbibe with caution. In fact, be careful with all of your mischiefs. I've seen summer associates not get jobs even though they did excellent legal work because they couldn't handle their alcohol or their impulses (or both) at firm events.

Everyone thinks it won't happen to them, until it does.

Fake it 'till you make it.

If you're a law student or a young lawyer, by definition you're inexperienced. I know it. You know it. Everyone knows it.

But that doesn't mean you should dwell on your inexperience. Or use your own inexperience as a crutch for the first few years of your career.

<u>You have to fake it until you make it.</u>

Let me give you a real-life example.

I once asked a summer associate, let's call him Bart, to research a question for me. Bart did the research and came back to me with the answer.

"Thanks," I said. "Do you want to draft the section of the federal district court summary judgment brief on this issue? Are you comfortable doing that?"

His response floored me. Not in a good way.

"I don't really feel qualified yet," Bart explained. "I haven't done that before."

I gave him a second chance, and really urged him to give it a try, to no avail.

"I shouldn't," was his answer.

I thought for a second that Bart was joking. He wasn't.

I then summoned a different summer associate, let's call her Lisa. I asked her the same question.

"Wow, really?" was Lisa's answer. "That'd be amazing."

Which summer associate do you think got hired full-time?

You need to train yourself to exude confidence. Apologizing for your inexperience is not going to make people want to hire you.

Be confident in your legal skills. Be confident in your own ability as a lawyer. If you aren't, your lack of confidence will shine through in your materials and in your interview. No one wants to hire an insecure lawyer.

Of course, it's fine to talk about your fears and insecurities; just don't do it too much with anyone in your professional circle or anyone who could hire you.

To be clear, I'm not saying you should act like a know-it-all. Or refuse to admit you don't know something. Honesty and candor are incredibly important in this line of work. I'm saying you need to act like you know what you're doing as a lawyer. Even if you don't.

The truth of the matter is that everyone feels like a fraud pretty much all of the way up until they retire—and especially when starting out in a new profession. It's OK. It just means you're human.

CHAPTER 3:
Figure Out Where You Stand in the Job Market

I hope that you're as glad as I am that the "Dear Abby" part of the book is over.

Now it's time to set your expectations. You need to figure out where you stand in the marketplace.

None of this is to say that you should not apply to jobs that are seemingly out of reach for you. <u>You can never apply too much or too often.</u> **Apply, apply, apply.**

Still, you need to at least have a basic understanding of your market value in order to make sure you are also applying to jobs that are likely to be interested in you.

How to figure out your rough market value.

It's surprisingly easy to do if you're in law school or if you graduated recently. It does, however, involve some basic math. (Sorry.)

Each year there are about 35,000 graduating law students.

To understand your market value, you need to figure out roughly where you fall in your group of 35,000 people who will graduate with you or already graduated with you.

Put another way, how do you compare to the lawyers (or law students) around the country who have the same seniority as you? Are you in the top 100, 1,000, 5,000, 10,000, etc.?

There are two primary factors that distinguish law students and recent graduates in the job market: class rank and school rank. Other things matter, of course. But those two are the big ones.

Below I've created a simple formula to help you figure out where you stand. Fill in your specific class rank and school rank details, take out your calculator, and solve for *Z*:

$$\left[\frac{\textit{Your law school's rank (1-200)}}{200}\right] \times [\textit{Your class rank percentage} \text{ (as a decimal point)}] \times 35{,}000 = \textbf{\textit{Z}}$$

For those of you who are mathematically challenged, I'll walk you through this.

First, you need to start with your law school's *U.S. News & World Report* ranking. Google it if you don't know it. It should be a numerical value falling somewhere between 1 and roughly 200 (because there are about 200 law schools).

If your law school is ranked 20th in the country, for example, then you'll need to divide 20 by 200 in the first part of the equation.

After you divide your law school's ranking by 200, write the resulting decimal point figure down. This is the percentage rank of your law school out of all law schools, expressed as a decimal point.

Again, for example, if your law school is ranked 20th, 20/200 = 0.1.

Next, it's time to figure out your class rank. Your class rank should be on your report card; if it's not, ask your school, and I'm sure they can give it to you (or at least they can give you a rough ballpark estimate).

Once you have your numerical class rank, you'll need to convert it into a percentage. To do that, divide your numerical class rank by the total number of law students in your law school class.

If you are ranked 50th in your law school class of 150, for example, you will get 0.33.

Finally, multiply your law school's rank as a decimal point (i.e., the first number you calculated) times your class rank percentage as a decimal point (i.e., the second number you calculated) times 35,000. That gives you your *Z*.

Write your *Z* down in the table on the next page.

The number *Z* represents a rough estimate of the number of people applying for jobs in your nationwide law school class who have a class rank percentage that is higher than yours **and** attend or

Z = The Approximate Number of Nationwide Applicants Ahead of You in Line for Jobs	

attended a law school that is ranked higher than yours.

How does this figure help you? Well, the number Z represents the "competitors" in your nationwide law school class who are going to be tough to beat out for jobs because, at least on paper, they will be ranked higher in their class at a higher ranked law school.

Next, consider approximately how many jobs are out there.

Job Type	*Approximate Number of Job Openings Per Year*
U.S. Supreme Court Clerkships	37
Federal Circuit Court Clerkships	500
Federal District Court Clerkships	1,000
AmLaw 100 Summer Associate Positions (2L)	5,500
AmLaw 100 First Year Associate Positions	4,500

These numbers might look big until you compare them with the approximate number of job seekers every year, 35,000.

Now compare your number Z (the one you wrote in the box) to the number of openings. If your number Z is 1,000, for example, you should have a pretty solid chance of landing a Biglaw summer associate position (assuming that's your goal). Of course, other factors matter too. And I'll talk about those later.

If your Z is higher than 10,000, however, maybe you shouldn't only focus on trying to land a 2L Biglaw summer association position. As I'll explain later, you should expand your search to smaller firms, government jobs, etc. You should also definitely start doing a lot of networking.

Of course, if you've been out of law school for a few years, you should also take your *Z* with a grain of salt. The further out you get from graduation, the less *Z* tells you.

That's because pretty quickly your job experience will start to weigh heavily into the calculus. As will the fact that, unlike in law school, not everyone in your class will be looking for a job at the same time.

You will therefore undoubtedly have a better chance of landing a job a few years out of law school, regardless of your class rank or school rank, simply because the applicant pool will be so much smaller and each applicant's experiences will be so much more diverse.

If, after doing the calculation above, you're feeling like dropping out or moving home and getting your old bartending job back, don't give up yet.

About 75% of you will end up employed as lawyers.

For many years, 75-95% of the graduates at the top 100 law schools have been employed within 10 months of graduating. And with a few exceptions, even 50-70% of the graduates at the law schools ranked between 150 and 200 have been employed as lawyers within 10 months of graduating.

That means, if you're in law school, it might take you some time to land a job. But it's *way* more likely than not that you'll find a legal job within a year of graduating.

On the other hand, if you graduated a few years ago and have been unemployed for a while, you still shouldn't worry: being unemployed is the new 30!

I kid. There is hope. Although the current ABA and BLS data I mentioned earlier shows that only 61% of all licensed lawyers are working as lawyers, those figures do not account for retired lawyers who are still licensed, people who don't want to work as lawyers, and people who don't need to work at all. The estimate is probably closer to 75% after adjusting for the unemployed lawyers out there who aren't looking for work.

<u>That means you only need to beat out about 25% of the other lawyers out there with your seniority to get a job.</u> Following the methods in this book, and sticking to them, will help you do that.

But before you start firing off resumes, there are a few basic, fundamental facts about your career as a lawyer that I need to make sure you understand.

These are things <u>all</u> law schools should be telling their students. Yet, based on my conversations with hundreds of recent law students, few of them are doing so.

CHAPTER 4:
What They Don't Tell You in Law School

So. Many. Damn. Things.
But let's start with the basics.

You will be your most marketable 3 to 5 years after passing the bar exam.

If you're a law student, you might be thinking: "So what? That's forever from now. And I need a job when I graduate."

This fact matters because you don't need to land your dream job or be in your preferred city in the first few years after you graduate.

That means you can cast a wide net when searching for jobs. Be as flexible as you possibly can.

Would you be willing to move to Miami, Florida for two years to work at a mid-sized law firm on the beach, for example, if you could end up where you want to live in three or four years doing your dream job?

Or would you agree to live in the middle of Kentucky working at a mid-sized regional law firm for a year in order to end up being a partner at an AmLaw 100 firm in your chosen city? (I did.)

You need your resume to be its strongest three to five years after you graduate. You can absolutely go from begging for jobs in law school to being annoyed by how many calls and emails you're getting from recruiters—all in a three- or four-year period. (And also, don't forget in five years if you're still in Miami and unhappy, it's time to get moving. ASAP).

Next...

Grades matter a lot but learning to write-well matters the most.

If you didn't notice the typo in that title, you should definitely read this sub-chapter. (There should not be a hyphen between the words "write" and "well.")

Like it or not, troves of judges, lawyers, and law professors measure a lawyer's skill based mostly on writing ability. (I'd bet money if some amazing newspaper writers were dropped into a law school exam, cold, they'd beat half the class.)

By writing, I don't mean IRAC, or whatever acronym they're teaching in legal writing classes now. I mean write well. Period. Don't screw up grammar. Don't have typos. Don't use commas unless you can't find another way to say it. Write clearly. Write concisely. Organize your writing with lots of headings and logical flow. And never, and I mean never, write a sentence that could be interpreted in two different ways.

I like to think that I didn't bring any bad writing habits to law school because I didn't have any writing habits at all.

In college I was a horrendous writer. I was placed into the lowest level "remedial" English class the first semester of my freshman year of college (their name for it, not mine). I did so poorly I got invited back for a second semester. I then went on to study economics and math.

I remember bragging to friends during my senior year of college that I only had to write two papers all year.

So, I guess I shouldn't have been so surprised when I took the GRE my senior year of college (because I thought I might want to get a master's degree), and I scored in the 25th percentile on the English section.

Put a less gentle way, 75% of the college seniors out there taking the GRE scored better than me in English. The year before I started law school.

Honestly, I believe this poor performance in college helped me when I got to law school. Writing wasn't my thing. And I knew it.

I had lots of objective reasons to think that my English skills needed a lot of work for me to succeed as a lawyer. So, I focused on writing more than anything else my first year in law school.

I went to the writing tutor after school. I read books on writing (both for lawyers and non-lawyers). I even bought a lawyer thesaurus. I just basically tried to consume as much information about writing as I could.

My knowledge that I sucked at writing may have been my savior. I never tried to delude myself into thinking I was a great writer. While others were focusing on their outlines, or trying to memorize their case books, I was trying to teach myself basic writing skills.

I ended up doing pretty well my first year in law school. I wasn't in the top ten percent, but I was squarely in the top twenty. I also made law review. I had no idea what I wanted to do my 2L summer. But I figured it wouldn't be too hard to land a job somewhere interesting with those stats.

Boy, was I wrong.

Which brings me to something else I had to learn on my own:

The more you get rejected, the better.

Get rejected as often as you can. Lean in. Enjoy it. Revel in it.

If you're in law school, get rejected by law review. Get rejected by moot court. Get rejected by your animal law clinic. Get rejected by 1,000s of firms and jobs before you graduate.

If you're a young lawyer, get rejected submitting articles to law journals. Get rejected when you seek a state bar board seat. Get rejected by your law firm's intramural ping pong team. Get rejected by conferences when you ask them if you can speak.

Get yourself rejected, smile, and then rinse and repeat.

The sooner you get over professional rejection, the better. As a lawyer, getting rejected is proof that you're trying hard. That's all it is.

Getting rejected is part of the profession. Being a lawyer means critiquing other people's writing and arguments. And being critiqued. All the time. For your entire career.

Some people aren't going to like your writing. Some people aren't going to like your legal arguments. Some people might not even like *you*. That's OK (as long as you're being a nice human).

I get rejected almost daily. When I send a draft contract, motion, or brief to a client, or co-counsel, I get back edits and criticisms of my arguments, tone, case strategy, even sometimes my clothes and facial hair (thanks, Zoom!).

Wear rejection as your badge of honor.

<u>You only need one "yes."</u> You only need one job you love. Think about that. You only need to convince one human (or maybe a small group of humans) to hire you.

There are 819,000 practicing lawyers in the U.S. Odds are pretty good you're going to find work. Your job now is to increase your opportunities, so you have more options later.

Increasing your leads and opportunities is good business. Keep doing it throughout your career, and you'll succeed.

Which leads to the next thing that no one explains in law school:

How the legal business works.

I spent three years in law school, and not once did anyone at my school explain how the business of law works. Probably because most law school faculty have no idea.

Why would they? It's not their business.

At my law school, there were no classes explaining how lawyers make money. There were no classes explaining how to write down time entries so clients will pay the bills. There were no classes even explaining the basic rate structure in law firms. Or explaining how partners get paid. Or explaining retainers, alternative fee arrangements, block billing, or even how to effectively use an assistant.

Learning these things gives you an advantage when you walk into any size law firm. You'll better understand, for example, why you shouldn't bother a partner with a question you can figure out on your own. (ANSWER: the partner's time is at least twice as expensive as yours, so if you can figure it out in a reasonable amount of time, that's better for the client and the partner.) You also won't drive the partners crazy when they are reviewing and editing bills before they go out to clients because your time entries will be perfect.

Understanding your job target's business will make you a much better applicant. It will allow you to ask more informed questions during your interview.

For example, you might ask a partner what their firm's average partner rates are.

Why do you care? A firm with higher partner rates is going to pay its partners more. Its partners will also have to bill less hours to make the same money as a partner at a firm with lower rates. But higher rates will also limit your ability to bring in lower-dollar work.

Maybe these things don't matter to you. That's fine. But asking about them in an interview shows you're smart and understand their business and the business of law.

"But I'm not planning to work at a firm," you might say. "So, why do I need to bother learning that boring stuff?"

Well, you should learn it because no one should be in a profession without a basic understanding of the economics of that profession. Unless you plan to work as a government lawyer your whole life, you need to understand these things (and even some government lawyers have budgets).

There are entire books written about the business of law. Buy one and read it. But in the meantime, Chapter 17 provides a crash course.

That brings me to a few things that I wish I knew while I was in law school that no one told me.

Author's Note: The next section is for 1Ls. The following two are for sub-100 ranked law students and top-tier law students looking to land Biglaw summer associate positions. If you don't fit those descriptions, you can skip to the three-star section break at the end of this chapter. In fact, I recommend it, because for some of you, knowing this information now when you can't do anything about it might piss you off. For example, when I was a 1L, I really wish I'd known the following.

Your 1L summer job doesn't matter.

Full stop. Don't let your gunner classmates or the law school's placement office convince you otherwise.

<u>You should never feel any stress about where you will work your first summer after starting law school.</u>

Work at McDonald's if you want. Or, even better, at your favorite non-profit. Or take classes. Or be a research assistant. Or go climb Mt. Kilimanjaro.

Why?

Because your 1L summer could be your last summer without any serious scholastic or professional stress and obligations for a while. Enjoy it.

No one at a firm expects you to have worked at a firm during your 1L summer. Firms don't hire a lot of 1Ls. No one does. So, if you land something, chalk it up as a bonus.

It's not, however, a serious detriment to your future to go home and live in your parent's basement for the summer, if you want.

My best shot at a 1L summer job was probably when I applied, unsolicited, to be a free summer intern at the local courthouse fifteen miles from my law school in Chelsea, Vermont. Population: a few hundred. They ghosted me.

I ended up taking environmental law classes in Vermont that summer and then driving across the country to visit national parks for five weeks. It was one of the best summers of my life. It also had zero impact on my career trajectory.

Which brings me to something else I wish I had known back then, especially as a rising 2L:

If you're at a sub-100 ranked law school, it is highly unlikely that you're going to land a Biglaw summer associate position.

Author's Note: This section is for the gunners at all the sub-100 ranked law schools. Everyone else can skip it. Or read it. Actually, forget I said anything. Just do whatever you want.

Even if you're ranked in the top five or ten of your class at a sub-100 ranked law school, unless you know somebody, are a movie star, or have a connection, Biglaw is—at best—a long-shot. And honestly, I doubt it.

My law school didn't tell me this. Based on my conversations with lots of law students and recent graduates, many current law schools and students are still clueless of this fact.

At the lowest ranked law schools, you have a minuscule, maybe not even measurable, chance of landing a Biglaw summer associate gig.

Don't believe me? Let's look at the stats again.

Statistically speaking, the average law student has about a 15% (or 1 in 7) chance of landing a 2L summer associate gig at a top 100 law firm.

A 15% chance might not sound too bad. But here's the thing: fifteen percent is the average across all law schools. The higher ranked law schools have much higher percentages, which means many lower ranked law schools are in the low single digits (or less) on a percentage basis.

Plus, if you're limiting your search to just summer associate positions in one or two of the more popular cities, or just the firms that come to your school's On-Campus Interviewing (OCI) program, your odds go down substantially. If, however, you expand your search to non-major market Biglaw offices, your chances will likely increase. (More on that later.)

Regardless, if you're at a lower-ranked law school and you want to work at a top firm, you don't necessarily have to work there as a 2L. In fact, lots and lots of people end up as partners at top law firms who did not have summer associate positions at those firms. For example, there are 25 lawyers in my Madison, Wisconsin Biglaw office. Only a handful of them were 2L summer associates at the firm.

Which brings us to our last law school secret, aimed at the elite...

It's OK if you go to a top 14 law school and don't get a 2L Biglaw summer associate position.

Author's Note: This section is for everyone at a top 14 law school. If that's not you, feel free to skip it unless you enjoy reading about the difficulties of the elite.

For those top 14 law school folks out there: at some point during your 2L year, likely in the fall, your friends and classmates will start landing 2L summer associate positions. And they'll talk about it a lot. I mean way more than anything else. I've heard this from many, many mentees at these schools.

It's understandable. It's exciting. The pay for 2L summer associate positions is high, especially in Biglaw, and the prestige the positions garner can be even higher.

Just remember this chatter is inevitable. Prepare for it.

Your classmates won't be able to help themselves. One of the most common things my mentees from higher-ranked law schools tell me is that they feel like failures because they didn't get a 2L summer associate position (either through their school's OCI program or otherwise). They think because they didn't get a 2L firm offer through OCI, that they'll never get a job. Or at least that landing a job at a firm is now hopeless.

All of this is wrong.

It's true that landing a 2L summer associate position at a law firm substantially increases your odds of landing a job right out of law school. But there are lots and lots of non-Biglaw firms out there that can provide you with a perfect platform to get where you want to be (yes, even if where you want to be is in Biglaw). More importantly, there are lots and lots of firms out there and offices of firms out there that did not participate in your school's OCI program.

You have to find these positions yourself.

* * *

Now that you know some of the key things you should have been told in law school, you're ready to implement my various schemes and strategies for getting hired.

I've done many of them myself. The others came from my mentees. Or from random people I've met over the years. Regardless, I recommend all of them.

CHAPTER 5:
Geography Matters

There's something important I need to tell you: geography matters.
Not the discipline that seeks an understanding of Earth and its human and natural complexities. I mean the physical locations *you are willing* to live in after you graduate.

Notice I said "willing." I did not say, "where you *want* to live."

Think carefully about where, geographically, you are willing to practice law for a few years.

You need to make a list. Write down the locations.
Why?
Because which cities and states you are searching for jobs in can significantly increase or decrease your odds of landing a job.

The geography analysis is much more complicated than just deciding to apply to your home state or city. You need to think it out. Strategize. And use your willingness to expand your geographical preferences as an advantage in your job search.

Don't just try to land jobs in New York City, Los Angeles, Chicago, and/or Washington D.C.

If you can, you should stay away from these job markets because they are the most competitive. The resume competition is *extremely* intense in these cities.

Is your resume going to stick out in a pile full of Harvard, Columbia, and N.Y.U resumes in New York City? Wouldn't you rather your resume be in basically any other pile of resumes?

Over 1,000 mentees have emailed me looking for mentors. That's a statistically significant number. Before I paired them up, I asked them all to tell me their preferred job location or locations.

About two-thirds of them responded with New York, Washington D.C., Chicago and/or Los Angeles.

If you have a personal reason requiring you to live in one of these cities, fine. If you have an ankle monitor and can't leave Chicago, or a significant other who can't (or won't) move, then limiting your job search to one of these locations might make sense.

Otherwise, trying to get a job only in these cities is a terrible approach. It is dead wrong. So wrong it could end up making it significantly harder for you to land your dream job.

Be as flexible as you can when picking geographies.

As lawyers, we have it pretty good when it comes to geography. We theoretically get to choose where we want to practice law.

A lot of other professions are not so lucky: I've known lots of PhD and medical students who had basically no choice where they were going to end up.

"A math professor job in eastern Kentucky? Sounds great!"

"A rotation in Topeka, Kansas? I can't wait!"

A lot of the law school folks reading this right now are probably planning to be an attorney in one particular city or state. If you're a badass, it might work out for you.

But for most people, uprooting and moving to a new place is easier to do earlier in their career, rather than later. So, if you're a law student or young lawyer you should at least seriously consider and analyze your geographic options.

In fact, everyone should look around geographically—or they risk selling themselves short. It's just a matter of degree for everyone.

There are lots of young lawyers, for example, who land big firm jobs in smaller cities who would not have been able to land a Biglaw job in a bigger city.

And it's not just a question of firms. In my experience, geography plays a significant role in marketability all the way up and down the line of job levels and types.

I've seen hustling, lower-ranked law school grads land agency jobs in small, less-sought-after cities after trying to land similar jobs for a year or more in Washington D.C. I've also seen people on the job hunt for a year or more start searching in a different, smaller market and almost immediately land a job.

You need to pick locations where your resume will stand out.

If you apply to firms and government agencies in Boston, for example, the people reviewing your resume are going to be used to seeing resumes from Harvard, Boston College, Boston University, and dozens of other nearby, highly ranked law schools.

If you apply to firms and government agencies in Portland, Oregon, however, they're going to be used to seeing resumes from Oregon, Lewis & Clark, and Willamette (all of which are awesome law schools, but not as highly ranked).

If you're a current law student at Cornell, where do you think your chances of landing a job will be better? Boston or Portland? This isn't rocket science, but lots of people never consider geography in their job search.

To get your dream job—or any job for that matter—you need to start your career by considering living in a place you might not have expected, at least for a few years.

Remember, you need to ensure that your resume ends up being in the top five of the pile if you want to have a decent shot at landing a position. If you aren't in the top five on paper (and don't have any other way in the door), you won't get a call. You might not even get a rejection letter or email. (From what I've heard, ghosting is apparently the norm now, which is a terrible thing.)

So, how can you help make sure that your resume is in the top five? <u>One way is to apply for jobs in cities or states surrounded by law schools with lower rankings than yours.</u>

Maybe instead of, or in addition to, shooting to land in New York City, you should target a city in a state like Florida. Sunny, beach-lined Florida has 21.5 million people and a dozen law schools—none of which rank higher than the University of Florida Law School (#21). By placing your focus on a state like Florida, you can boost your chances of scoring an interview and eventually landing a job.

Of course, if you went to a law school ranked 190th and can't compete with University of Florida grads, there are still options. Maybe try focusing on states without a top 100 law school, such as Delaware, Idaho, Maine, Montana, New Mexico, North Dakota, Rhode Island, South Dakota, West Virginia, Wyoming, and Vermont.

The truth is that if you pick the right locations, you could end up at an AmLaw 100 firm when you wouldn't have otherwise gotten that same job in a bigger city. Or you could land a great state clerkship that you never would have otherwise been able to land.

If you end up at a well-respected firm in Montana after graduating, for example, two or three years later if you don't love your job <u>or your geography</u>, you can move to your dream job. At that point, you'll have a much better-looking resume at a time when you are much more marketable.

I don't know about you, but I wouldn't have minded living in South Beach for a few years after law school in order to get a leg up.

Narrow your list down to five locations.

Make a list of the places you'd be willing to live. Pick five to focus on. <u>And make sure at least three of those five are not New York City, Chicago, Washington D.C., or LA.</u>

Choose geographies like you chose law schools. Pick a few geographies that are your safety schools, so to speak. If you're from Tennessee, pick Nashville and Memphis even if you'd prefer to be in Chicago and DC. If you're from New York City, pick Albany, Syracuse, or Boston (if you can stomach the Red Sox fans).

Give yourself a real chance—don't just shoot for the moon.

And after narrowing down your list, you can move on to the fun part: networking in those cities.

CHAPTER 6:
Network, Network, Network

You've got your list of locations. Now your task, whether you like it or not, is to meet lots of lawyers in those locations.

One of the most important professional steps that any living human can take—and yes, us lawyers are living human beings—is to network.

The bottom line is that the name of this chapter says it all: network, network, network. <u>Growing your network is essential to your professional, and thus, personal, success.</u>

One cannot possibly overstate the importance of networking. The world of law is very much about who you know—especially when it comes to landing a job. And if you get lucky and make the right connections, in a few years you could land a great job. Maybe you'll even beat out a few Grade A law school grads from top-ranked law schools with enough capital in the bank to launch their own hedge funds.

I'm not saying that you need to be a schmoozer. Don't be annoying. That isn't going to help you. But a quick meeting, followed-up with a drop-in email or text from time to time never hurt anyone—especially if the contact that you've created is genuine and authentic.

In this chapter, we're going to go a bit more in-depth about some networking methods you can use to further—or jumpstart—your career. And the best part? You don't even need to leave your couch.

Zoom has changed the world.

While video chatting was obviously around pre-pandemic, it has never been more widely used, more accessible, and more convenient than it is today. With that in mind, it has become even easier for aspiring lawyers and young lawyers to build their networks by Zooming with practicing attorneys, attending virtual conferences, webinars, courses, and so much more.

Everyone is accessible. Absolutely everyone. This isn't some phenomenon either. It's reality. The world is virtual, so naturally you should network virtually too. I'm not just talking about connecting with a few lawyers on LinkedIn. I mean really immersing yourself in the field and meeting new people who can help you get hired.

Oh, and there's one more thing that Zoom has done. It's made travel costs to meet with people irrelevant. No hotel stays. No plane tickets. No restaurant bills. Just plain, simple, and ordinary visual networking at its best.

Getting started isn't the hardest part.

Usually, the hardest part about doing anything is getting started. Yet many of the job seekers I've spoken with didn't have any problem getting started networking; they had a hard time keeping with it.

I've heard so many mentees tell me that they've emailed "lots" of people to try to set up networking meetings. When I ask how many, it's usually twenty to thirty people. They might have actually met via video or in-person with only one or two of them (if any). But they gave up trying because it wasn't working and was too time consuming. (I'll explain why this is dead wrong later.)

Networking is something that you'll need to build into your routine. Make it a habit, because once you get the wheels turning, it gets easier and easier. You'll start to feel comfortable. You'll start to open up. You'll start to show people just who you are as a person and a professional—and that's what will get you hired in the end.

What you want is to build a snowball effect. Make sure your networking is always expanding to add new people. Soon you'll always have someone available if you want to do something. And the more people you know—and that know you—the better your chances are of landing your dream job two, five, ten or twenty years from now.

Your five networking goals.

I have five simple goals to help you get started and keep you on the right track.

> *Goal 1: Zoom with two to three different,*
> *new professional acquaintances each week.*
> *Total Time Commitment: 1.5 hours per week*

Don't worry. All of these people won't be moving in next door to you. You can't and won't be able to keep in touch with all of them. It's up to you to determine who you click with and want to keep in touch with.

I'll tell you how to get all these new people to meet with you in the next chapter. For now, all you need to know is that this is your goal. I'll repeat it for emphasis: Zoom with two to three <u>different</u> new people each week. Not phone calls. Video chats.

They can be with people from where you live. Or with lawyers in a city you're thinking about moving to. It doesn't matter.

Keep the first meetings to 15-20 minutes—30 minutes tops—even if you're really hitting it off.

This might sound like a big burden. But it amounts to only 1.5 hours of your time per week. You can make room for it.

> *Goal 2: Get two new contacts from each of your video meetings.*
> *Total Time Commitment: 0 hours*

At the end of every video meeting with these new contacts, say the following (even if you hated them). Write it out on a sticky note if you have to.

"This has been great! Thank you so much for meeting with me. I've learned so much from you!!!"

Now here's the trick. Pay attention.

Next, ask them to share one or two of their contacts with you.

"If you know other people I could talk to in town, I'd love a recommendation or two."

Just one or two. Don't ask them to email you their entire contact list.

And try not to be a weirdo when you ask. If you do it right, it will feel totally natural; it won't be awkward at all.

Hell, I'm fine if you say:

"I read this terrible book called The Jobless Lawyer's Handbook. *It's about how to get a job. It was really, really bad. But it did have one tip I liked. The book recommended that you ask for one or two contacts at the end of each meeting like this. I do it every time now. Do you have a contact or two you can share with me that I can follow up with?"*

Basically, all you have to do is give an honest reason why you would like to meet some of their contacts.

Here's another one that works well:

"I'm thinking about moving to Dallas [or wherever this person is from]. Would you mind referring me to one or two people who might be willing to give me some more advice about which litigation departments are the best to work for in the city?"

Make sure to tweak this text for your own situation or you're going to sound crazy talking to the corporate legal department of a Boston law firm.

Almost everyone will give you contact information. Because they want to help. And now, when you email those new people to ask for a quick Zoom meeting, say the following in the first sentence:

"I got your name from [so-and-so]."

Ta-daaaah! You've just created your own warm introductions out of thin air.

> *Goal 3: Go to at least one in-person social outing*
> *with a lawyer or business contact per week.*
> *Total Time Commitment: 1 hour per week*

Not people you currently work with (in the unlikely event you have a job). That's the only rule.

Lunch. Coffee. Dinner. Cocktails. Whatever you like to do. Do it and invite someone.

In a year or less, this goal will be easy to meet. You'll have made so many contacts you like that there will always be someone to grab coffee or lunch with. (Or to go to the bar with.)

Making yourself meet with another professional at least once a week forces you to be consistent; networking is like running—you need to do it routinely to enjoy it and to be any good at it. That means do not under any circumstances skip this rule for a few weeks because you're studying for the bar, searching the internet all day for job postings, or going out too much to the clubs.

This goal is about nurturing your existing contacts and making friends. Once a week you have to do something fun with a lawyer or businessperson you know. That's it. It should be an easy—even automatic—rule to meet.

Location and setting don't matter as long as you can (and do) talk to each other. Try not to have other colleagues around. One on one is preferable. But a small intimate group is OK too.

> *Goal 4: Do something nice for at least*
> *two professional contacts each week.*
> *Total Time Commitment: 1 hour per week*

As a young lawyer, you naturally are going to need more help than you can give. People know that. They don't expect any favors. Which is wonderful. But the sooner you start helping your contacts achieve their goals, the better your networking results will be.

Sometime in my second or third year as a law firm associate, I learned that sales is about doing nice things for other people with no strings attached. People who you help today will want to help you tomorrow. Period. It really is that easy.

I've taken that knowledge to heart, and it's worked well for me. Every time I meet with someone and learn about what they're currently doing, I look for ways to help them.

If they just moved to a new city, I'll tell them about a great restaurant there, and I'll email-introduce them to a friend I like that lives there. If they work at a law firm doing privacy law, I'll email them about a cool privacy conference that they might be interested in attending. If they are looking to hire a third-year associate, and I know of a good candidate, I'll refer that person to them. You get it. Do nice things to others and nice things will happen to you.

Set aside an hour or so a week to really sit down and think about ways to do this. Then do them.

Of course, as a law student or recent grad with a limited network, figuring out ways to help others will be tricky. What does a tenth-year partner need from a rising 2L, after all? But the answer is that everyone can use some help. Even if it's something small; it's the thought that counts.

To be clear, I'm not talking about sending them a thank you letter in the mail for talking to you. Gifts and cards are nice. But if you take the time to actually do something that might help them live a happier life, grow their professional network, and/or increase their chances of professional success, you will always be remembered.

Goal 5: Don't ever stop meeting Goals 1 through 4.

Everyone should start networking in law school, preferably their first year. Then they shouldn't stop. Not ever. Not after landing a summer associate position; not after landing a job; not even ten (or fifteen) years later after finally landing a dream job.

Lawyers are consultants. Consultants have to know people to succeed. Who you know and interact with, and how you treat them now, will impact your career in five or ten years. Your law school and other low-on-the-totem pole friends and confidants now could easily be in places that can help you succeed in a decade. They'll want to help you then because you've networked with them and done nice things to help them over the years. Remember that.

Keep your first networking meetings short, no matter what.

Your meeting is running long. Your self-imposed 30-minute limit is about to expire. The person doesn't seem like she wants to stop talking to you.

What do you do?

This is not a trick question. You end the meeting. Force it to end if you have to.

Why? Because you don't know this person well enough to gauge whether they are good at giving you the "I want to get off the Zoom" signal. You have to be respectful of their time.

So, how do you do this smoothly? At the 27 or 28 minute mark, you say:

"I have to go. Sorry to cut this short."

Or, "I have another meeting I need to get to right now. But this has been great!"

And then, of course, you ask the person to share two of their contacts with you.

CHAPTER 7:
How to Get People to Meet with You

Ask them. It's that easy.

Start with people you know well.

A few times a year, I get asked for marketing advice. Usually, it's from a senior associate at my firm who suddenly realizes that they should try to get clients.

That's what partners are supposed to do, right?

(Actually, there are lots of firm partners who don't get clients; they're called service partners; basically, they're good enough at lawyering that they don't need their own clients.)

I, of course, meet with any marketing mentee that asks for advice. (I always meet with anyone who asks for advice, and you should too—write that down.)

We set aside an hour. But before the person shows up, I tell them to print off a list of all their LinkedIn connections. I tell them to go through the list and highlight anyone who might be able to give them work today or anytime within the next ten to twenty years.

When they show up, almost everyone has a decent-sized list.

We then talk about each person on their list in detail. Where do they work? How do they know each other? Basically, why are they on the list?

Then together we figure out ways to reconnect with each person.

Why do I do this and not focus on conferences they could go to, boards they might be able to get on, or articles they could write to get their names out there? Because, again, lawyers are consultants. And consulting is a relationship-based business.

Getting a job is marketing. You're marketing yourself. And your best helpers are the people who already know you. The people who (hopefully) like you.

Scour your LinkedIn, Instagram, and Facebook connections. Get out your rolodex (if you're old school).

Make a list of everyone you know who works at a company or law firm that could hire you. Also include people who just know a lot of other professionals. Lawyers, non-lawyers, your cat sitter. Basically, anyone working. Be overinclusive.

Then go through them one at a time. Think about whether each person might know someone who can help you land a job. Put them in an order of priority that makes sense.

Next, email them and get them to meet with you. In person or via Zoom.

I'll talk about spam emails soon. These aren't those.

Email your college friend who works as an entry-level accountant at Frito-Lay, for example. Or that high-school buddy working at a startup.

Hopefully you don't need me to tell you what to say to these people you already know. (If you do, you should probably keep this book with you at all times.)

Still, I'll tell you anyway, just be safe.

Just say: "Hey, you want to grab lunch at that new Mexican place?" Or "Hey, I have some recent news that I'd love to share with you. Have ten minutes for a quick Zoom call?"

Basically, say whatever you want.

Then go to lunch. Or Zoom with them. Catch up. See how they're doing. Have fun. Your job hunt doesn't always have to be stressful.

You only have a few goals with each encounter. Those are:
1. Make sure you tell them you're on the job hunt.
2. Ask them if they've heard of any job openings that might be a good fit.
3. Pick their brains on how best to expand your job search. (One

can never get too much advice.)
4. Ask them if they know anyone who might be good for you to talk to.

They may not have a job lead for you. You might leave lunch empty-handed. That's OK. You're creating opportunities. Which is the name of the game.

Follow this procedure with your professional contacts and friends as early, and then often, as you can. In-person and Zoom meetings are the best. But if you can't fit in enough coffee and lunch meetings, then call them and do the same thing.

You want as many of your friends and professional contacts as possible to know you are on the job hunt. These folks will be your allies; they will immediately extend your web.

Next, turn to warm leads and more attenuated acquaintances.

Use your solid connections to make warm introductions for you. That's the easiest way to get meetings with people you don't know well.

If your Frito-Lay friend knows someone at a law firm, for example, ask her to introduce the two of you via email. If your dad knows a lawyer or two, get him to introduce you.

If you don't know who your friends and family know, ask them. Just say, "Would you go through your contact list and give me one or two people you know who might be good for me to meet and network with?"

Most people who like you will do this for you and feel great about it.

Turn next to people who you've met but don't know well. This can also be very effective.

Maybe a few lawyers came to your law school to judge your moot court competition last month. Email them. Lead with how you know them. Then ask them for advice about something. Literally anything.

I know it can be hard to make the leap and ask someone you just met or don't know well to have lunch.

But hey: What's the worst thing that will happen? They reject you. They ghost you. So what?

Rejection is something you have to get proficient at handling. You can't let your fear of rejection keep you from making friends and professional acquaintances who might ultimately help you land your dream job.

Tap into your law school's job resources.

As limited as they are.

Don't get me wrong. I loved law school. I learned new, mostly useful information every day. It was challenging. I met amazing people.

While law schools aren't perfect, they generally do a solid job of teaching people how to think and act like a lawyer. They provide students with the resources and tools to succeed. They open doors. And they ultimately give you a degree that will increase your overall value in the job market.

I've always said that education is a good thing, no matter the expense. They can't put you in jail for failing to pay back your law school loans. (That fact kept me well-fed and well-endowed with technology in law school.) Most importantly, they can't foreclose on your brain.

But don't kid yourself: most law schools are focused on providing you with a good legal education—and preparing you for the bar exam—not on teaching you how to build a career as a lawyer.

The tools, however, are generally available. You just need to seek them out.

Whether you're in law school or recently graduated, tap into every law school job resource that you can: law professors, your law school's placement office, alumni, and anyone else you can find along the way. Most of these people would love to help you, even if you've already graduated.

Talk to them about your career. Ask for advice. Ask them what they would do in your shoes. People love to give advice (some people love it so much they even write lame "how to" books).

Law professors are the easiest to approach. It's their job to help you. But remember, a lot of tenured law professors have never practiced law. Or if they did practice, they did so for only a few years.

Unfortunately, their ability to give real world advice is therefore often limited.

That's not to say your law professors didn't work hard to get to where they are. But I seriously doubt that many needed to claw their way to the top of the legal profession. A very high percentage of tenured law school faculty graduated from a top 10 law school. Getting a job was pretty much a given for them after graduating from college.

Still, law professors generally care about their current and former students. They want their students to succeed. They want them to get jobs. They'll do what they can to help you land a job. Use that.

Law school placement offices are also generally filled with helpful people who have your best interest in mind. Their job is to find you a job. So, don't be shy. Ask for what you need. If you get resistance or grumpiness, gently push back and endure. I guarantee you are not the most annoying student or former student they've ever dealt with. Not even close.

Still, keep in mind that law professors and law school placement professionals are often limited in what they can recommend because they need to consider their law school's reputation. They aren't likely to tell you to spam associates and partners at law firms, for example, because they might be worried that such tactics will reflect poorly on their school. They aren't likely to tell you to do some of the more dramatic things I recommend in this book for the same reason.

I, on the other hand, couldn't care less about how your job search impacts your law school. I'm not going to tell you to do anything unethical, stupid, or illegal. But your job search is about you. Not protecting your school. Not protecting your law professors. Not protecting your law school's alumni.

Getting a great job should be at or near the top of the list of things you care about. Prioritize it as such.

Once you've tapped into the people you know and your law school's resources, it's time to...

Use LinkedIn to expand your network.

First, start by connecting with Brian H. Potts.

No, seriously, connect with me.

I'll accept your connection request because I accept all connection requests. Then message or email me. Ask to meet with me if you want (I never say no to such requests). Or just email me and ask for some lawyer mentors.

Hopefully I'll be able to give you other practicing lawyers to connect with. Maybe I'll even know someone who can hire you. Maybe not.

Then scour my 16,000+ LinkedIn connections. Start connecting with my connections. And off you go.

LinkedIn is one of the most powerful networking tools out there. It's great for meeting new people. You can search for people in certain jobs, connect with them, and if they accept, you can message them through LinkedIn or get access to their email address.

You can go through your connections' connections. Connect with interesting ones. Ask for advice via Zoom.

You can like and/or reply to posts of other professionals. Be supportive. Then message them and take the discussion off-line. You can even post your articles and other content on LinkedIn.

To be sure, you aren't likely to make long-term bonds with people by communicating with them only over LinkedIn. But the platform gives you access to basically any professional anywhere in the world.

Use that feature to gin up leads to sell yourself to or network with.

You can also join some seriously nerdy LinkedIn groups, and then network through those groups. Want to go into Energy Law? There's a LinkedIn group for that!

Remember that there is someone for everyone.

My way of handling professional relationships may be a little naïve. But it works.

Be nice and respectful to everyone. Always.

Just remember that people are different. They have different beliefs, emotions, feelings, personalities, and principles. It would be weird if everyone liked you; lots of people don't like me. That's fine. I'm OK with it because I'm not sure there is anyone alive who everyone likes. Or at least that's what I tell myself. I try to get along with everyone. But if someone doesn't like me, I'm fine with it. You should be too. It's very freeing.

Some people easily make friends; others don't. However, there's someone for everyone. I truly believe that. Everyone, and I mean everyone, can find a few people they mesh with. You might have to work harder at it if you're a raging introvert that loves reading fantasy novels and building model trains. But anyone can build a network. Even you.

Just bother people to find the right people.

Maybe your fear isn't rejection. Maybe it's imposing on other people's time. Don't go there either.

<u>You're never imposing on someone by asking them if they want to get coffee or lunch with you.</u>

Obviously don't ask them ten times in a row if they keep saying no. But you should assume that if someone does not want to do something with you, they will either tell you they don't want to or will make up an excuse.

What matters, however, is that they will never like you less because you showed an interest in them.

How to further expand your network.

Maybe all these meetings with your existing connections and the people you meet through LinkedIn will bear fruit. If they do, great. You did it. But you should keep reading on because the chances that you just landed your last job, and it's your dream job, are very low.

You need to keep expanding your network.

Don't get dissuaded if networking through your existing connections doesn't land you any interviews or jobs. This is just the beginning of your search.

Your goal is to expand your opportunities. The more you do that, the higher your chances are of getting a job.

To really expand your network, you need to meet lawyers you've never met before. Lots of them.

I'll tell you how to do that in the next chapter.

CHAPTER 8:
Spam, Spam, Spam

Author's Note: Please don't tell any of my law firm partners about this chapter. Thank you.

Why you should spam a lot.

Spam (i.e., unsolicited and random emails, not the salty meat that comes from a can) is the best way for law students and recent graduates to generate meetings with lawyers they don't know.

All you need to do is dedicate some mind-numbing time in front of a computer finding relevant email addresses and spamming everyone interesting you find.

Spam a few hundred people in an afternoon, and you're bound to get more than a few meetings.

Of course, every spam-induced meeting isn't going to lead to a job. But one might. And every meeting is an opportunity.

I wish it weren't this way. I wish there were an easier way to connect. But you need to put yourself out there, and the easiest way to engage people is to email them. (Messaging through LinkedIn can work too; but very few lawyers regularly check their LinkedIn messages.)

To be clear, spamming people you don't know will probably feel weird and invasive. It should. That makes you a normal, nice person. But you need to get over those feelings.

Most of the time, spamming people feels weird to you, but not to them. Everyone I know gets spammed. All the time.

If anything, a spam from a real human is a nice change of pace. Hey look: a real person wants to connect with me!

An email or two asking for advice is usually not even going to break someone's stream of thought. No one will remember your spam if they don't respond to it. No one.

Of course, you might get a few snide comments from unhappy lawyers looking to vent. But they aren't going to call you. Or track you down and beat you up.

Lawyers are too busy for any of that.

How to find lawyer email addresses.

To spam people, you need an email address that someone regularly checks. For some types of lawyers, finding their email address is easy. For others, there's more work involved.

Law firm lawyers put their email addresses everywhere they can: on their website, on their business cards, on their shirt sleeve, on billboards around town.

You can therefore find private lawyer emails with almost no work: just go to a law firm's website, search by professional or practice area, and you'll find email addresses for most, if not all, of the firm's lawyers.

If you need to find a bunch of law firm lawyer email addresses in Seattle, for example, just Google "Seattle law firms." Make a list of all of them you can find. Then go to each of their websites to find relevant professionals. You can almost always search by practice area and geography. Sometimes you can even search by schools attended.

Finding in-house and government lawyer contacts, however, can be much trickier. How would you go about finding an email address for an in-house counsel at Nike, for example? Or for lawyers who work at a particular state agency?

Let me tell you.

First, I'll start with the easiest way: connect with them on LinkedIn. Once you're connected, you'll usually immediately get access to their email address. It's that simple.

Just search LinkedIn by pairing an agency or company name

with the words "attorney" or "counsel." Then scroll through the results (you may want to subscribe to LinkedIn Premium if your results are too limited.)

Search for "counsel" and "Nike" on LinkedIn, for example. Connect with a few. Then if they accept your connection request, *viola!* You've got their email address. Just scroll down through their bio and there's usually an email address available.

Again, you might think it's creepy to connect with people you don't know. It's not. LinkedIn isn't Facebook or Instagram. You don't have to know the other person to connect. Of course, lots of people won't accept your connection request. Just like lots of people won't respond to your spam emails. But lots and lots of people will connect with you.

Pro-tip: Don't go too crazy connecting with random people or LinkedIn will lock your account. If you connect with less than 20 or 30 people a day, however, you should be fine.

For government lawyer email addresses, you can use the LinkedIn trick too. But many states also have state employee contact directories. You can search by position. Or you can search LinkedIn, find the names of people who work at state agencies, and then go search the state's directory by name.

Most of the federal agencies have their own directories too. So, you can follow the same process. Or worst case, if you can't find them online, you could always just submit a Freedom of Information Act (FOIA) request and make the agency send you a current roster of its attorneys and their contact information.

How many spam emails should you send?

Hundreds. Maybe thousands.

I tell people to expect a 1% response rate. That means if you send 100 emails, expect one response. I don't have any actual empirical data to back up my 1% figure; it just feels right as an assumption.

Some mentees have reported 1% response rates to me. Others received responses from 10-15% of the people they emailed. No one has ever told me anything higher than 15%.

That means the best-case scenario is that 85% of people are ignoring requests for advice from law students and young lawyers, which is sad.

Even so, while there are a lot of self-centered, egotistical assholes out there who don't want to commit time to anything other than themselves, there are also still plenty of people out there willing to help.

Your job is to find those people.

Spamming 101.

The next chapter tells you how to write the perfect cold, spam email. Before we get there, however, I need to set a few guidelines:
1. <u>Don't email more than one person at a time.</u> You want your spam to feel personal. Emailing a lot of people at the same firm on the same email tells them immediately that you are bothering a big group of people. On the other hand, if you spammed me, and then separately spammed everyone else in my office, it's unlikely I would know you emailed everyone else. So, do that.
2. <u>Don't email the same person more than twice.</u> If email number one goes unanswered, it's OK to follow-up two weeks later and say something like:

    > *"Just putting this at the top of your email box. I met with someone at [X-Y-Z law firm] last week, and he gave me some great advice about litigation firms in town. I would still love to meet with you too and get some additional insights if you've got 15 or 20 minutes to spare."*

    If they don't respond to the second nudge, leave them alone.

3. <u>Don't spam via LinkedIn messenger if you have their email address.</u> Work email is better than personal email, is better than LinkedIn messenger, is better than Twitter DM, is better than any other social media contact.

Unfortunately, spamming needs to happen. Just do it gracefully, and—if you've got it in you—with pizazz. Treat people like they're humans first and lawyers second.

CHAPTER 9:
The Cold Email

My wonderful wife, Abigail, ran for county board supervisor in 2017—and she won! It was her—and by association my—first experience with politics.

At the beginning, we thought it would be fun. Overall, it was. Parts of the campaigning process, however, were pretty miserable. In particular: calling people for money and knocking on doors.

Abigail did most of the dialing for dollars. I helped with knocking on doors.

Together we knocked on well over two thousand doors during one of Wisconsin's coldest winters ever recorded.

Other than having to bundle up and deal with the frigid temperatures, the process was pretty simple.

We got an address list of people who voted in the last election. We then went out to neighborhoods, split up, knocked on the pre-identified doors, and told whoever would listen that they should vote for Abigail.

Knocking on doors initially made me feel terrified and embarrassed. I was nervous. I was self-conscious about bothering people.

I eventually got over these feelings. But it took some time.

Emailing people cold, without any prior connection, is like knocking on doors. It feels uncomfortable and invasive.

It should at first. That's OK. Everyone feels that way. But you can't let that feeling keep you from putting yourself out there.

To get elected, most people need to knock on some doors. To get a job, most people need to cold email some people.

At first, when I started knocking on doors, I always led with an apology. When someone came to the door, I'd say something like: "I'm sorry to bother you on a weekend." Or "I know it's cold outside, but I just need a minute of your time."

Doing this made me feel better. But I quickly figured out that leading with an apology put me on the defensive and led to less fruitful interactions.

In other words, knocking on doors worked better when I ignored the oddity of it and dove right into why I was there and what I needed.

Cold emailing people is the same. Don't lead with an apology. Lead with what you need. And, definitely...

Always ask for advice, not a job.

When you email people cold, don't ask for a job and attach your resume. The word "job" should never appear in any of your cold emails. This is not an optional recommendation.

Ask for advice. Always. <u>Advice, advice, advice.</u>

<u>Not a job! Don't even say the word "job." Never say "job" (unless you're applying to a job opening).</u>

If you're interested in litigation, tell them you're interested in litigation and you want to know who the best litigators are in the city they live in. Or ask them which firms are the best to work for where they live.

It doesn't matter what kind of advice you seek. It just needs to be plausible.

To help you not have to think as much, I've provided a couple samples below. Feel free to plagiarize them at will.

> *"Hi! My name is Emily, and I'm a 2L at the University of Kentucky College of Law. I'm from Texas, but I'm interested in moving to Nashville after graduation and doing patent litigation. I'm looking for some intel about patent litigation firms in Nashville. Would you be willing to hop on a short Zoom call with me to give me the lay of the land? I'd really appreciate your insights. Thanks!"*

Or, you could try:

"Hello! My name is Carlos. I'm a law student from Spain currently pursuing an LL.M degree at Duke. I'm planning to move to Miami and practice corporate law after I graduate. Unfortunately, I don't know any lawyers in Miami. Would you be willing to chat with me for a few minutes to give me some advice about which firms have the best corporate practices in Miami? Thanks for your consideration."

Asking for advice rather than a job will lead to more people responding to your unexpected emails. Why? Because when you ask for a job, or even imply that landing a job is your main goal, lots of people won't talk to you unless they can give you a job. They'll just ignore your email and feel guilty. Or they'll ignore your email and never give it a second thought. Either way, you'll get nothing from them.

Yet, you can get so much useful information from people who can't give you a job. References to other people to seek advice from, for one. Hidden or upcoming job openings in town, for another. They might also give you tidbits about the culture at their employer and/or at other employers in their town. Who knows? Maybe in a few months they'll lose an associate and email you to see if you're still hunting for a job.

Ask for advice, not a job.

Be nice. And good things will happen.

Try to find a connection, and lead with that.

Search the internet and scour firm websites for people who share a school, geography, or interest with you.

Then start your cold email with "Hi _____, I'm a recent University of Wisconsin, Madison grad"—if they're also an alum. Or put "I'm an LL.M student from Mexico City," as your email heading, if you're both from Mexico City.

It could be your undergrad or your past employers that connect you. Great, use it. However you are able to link yourself to them, do that in the first sentence of the cold email. It'll greatly increase your chances of a response.

If you don't have anything else, then lead with something catchy.

For example, you could try these, which would probably get some responses:

To: Stewie Griffin
Subject: Help Wanted!
I'm a law student looking for a labor and employment lawyer to tell me about the profession. Please help.

Or flattery always works:

To: Eric Cartman
Subject: Your biography is impressive.
I'm trying to figure out which Miami firms have the best litigation departments. And you seem like the perfect person to talk to about it.

Who wouldn't look at and respond to those emails? I would.
Or, if you're only a little adventurous, you could just be honest:

To: Liz Lemon
Subject: I'm a law student seeking some advice.
Would you be willing to give me a few minutes of your time? I am new to the area and would be incredibly grateful.

Basically, be creative. Take the time to think about whether your email will interest people. Remember that it is possible to say and get what you want without being boring about it.

For those of you, on the other hand, who might be thinking about tricking people into meeting with you...

Do it! (Please don't.)

Seriously! Why not?! What could go WRONG?! (A lot.)

Let's be real. You're feeling frantic. Why else would you read a jobless lawyer's handbook?(Hey now!)

If you send this email to a few law firm partners, they'd definitely respond. (I'm obligated to instruct you not to send this email.)

To: Elle Woods
Subject: Looking for counsel.
Do you have time to chat for a few minutes via Zoom?

A few more hot tips for those cold emails.

1. Keep your emails very—and I mean *very*—short.
   Use only four or five sentences.
2. No typos or grammatical errors are allowed.
   The moment your recipient spots something that doesn't look right or feel right, they'll move right on to the next spam email in their inbox.
3. Avoid commas where possible.
   I hate commas. As do most lawyers. Avoid them if you can.
4. Be careful with over-capitalization.
   I'm not sure where law students and recent grads are picking up the habit, but Rampant and Random capitalization seems to be the Norm. Don't do it.

CHAPTER 10:
How to Perfect Your Resume

Everything I've told you thus far about networking, geography, and career planning is more important to your career search than what's on your resume. I truly believe that. It's why I put that stuff first in the handbook.

Still, your resume obviously matters. It's the one thing you give prospective employers that they will definitely look at before deciding whether to hire you (unlike your writing sample and cover letter, which I'll cover in the next chapter). <u>Just don't ever forget that you matter more than what's on your resume.</u>

Understand how your resume fits into the hiring process.

I've hired quite a few people. After posting a job, sometimes you get lots of resumes. Sometimes you don't.

Regardless, you end up with a pile to look through. (Sometimes pruned by the recruiting department, if you have one.)

Then what?

Well, you look at all the resumes. You put aside at least two and probably less than five. You almost definitely never look at the rest again.

This process is the same everywhere. Someone narrows down the pool. And they're doing it based on your resume.

Your resume therefore HAS TO STAND OUT.

Of course, I can't make your resume have better credentials; but I *can* show you how to make your resume more persuasive, more salient, and more likely to land in that critical top-five candidate pool.

Look at your resume the right way.

Building your resume from the first line down starts with looking at it the right way. You want to look at your resume as if you were a potential employer.

What would you want to see on a top candidate's resume? What credentials would you want them to have? What level of experience? How does the resume look? Is it long? Short? Too much irrelevant information? Too little critical information? All of these factors matter, and you need to consider each of them individually and holistically.

The bottom line is this: your credentials are what they are. I can't waive a wand and change your law school to Yale and your undergrad to MIT.

But I can help you tell your story in the most compelling way possible. And, perhaps most importantly, I can make sure your resume does not unnecessarily raise red flags, which could cost you an opportunity at securing an interview.

The one-page resume rule is stupid.

If your law school recruiting folks tell you that your resume needs to be one page or less, thank them for their advice. Then ignore their advice.

There's only one rule as to length: don't make the reader read for no reason. Include all relevant and impressive information. Nothing more, nothing less.

No one cares if your resume is one, two, three, or even four pages long; what matters is whether you've got good things on it.

How to make the education section pop.

Your educational background, for the post part, is what it is.

The Jobless Lawyer's Handbook: How to Get Hired as a Lawyer

Still, there are some strategies that can help.

If you have stronger work experience than educational experience, for example, put your work experience first on your resume. And vice versa.

If you were in the top ⅓ of your law school class, say so. Otherwise, don't.

If you graduated with a high GPA in college, list your GPA. If you made Dean's List every semester in college, say so. If you only made it once, don't.

Don't go overboard with college accolades. For the most part, no one will care what you did in college, so keep your college section short. Two to four bullet points is fine.

If you went to a college or law school that no one has heard of, in the first bullet explain where the school is and what is great about it.

If you studied IP in law school but are applying for a corporate position, explain why on your resume when talking about your IP law school background.

Basically, look at your education section and make sure everyone who looks at it will know everything they need to know about *why* your educational background is impressive.

To make it easy for you, here are the *only* things I recommend including in the law school section:

- GPA and class rank (only if in the top ⅓)
- Law review & journal memberships
- Moot court and trial competitions
- Leadership positions in groups
- Top grade awards
- Teaching assistant positions
- Publications

Anything not on this list is usually wasting space and the reviewer's time.

For example, <u>I do not recommend listing classes taken on your</u>

resume. Most practicing lawyers won't care what classes you took in law school. If you got the highest grade in a class, say that. But the fact that you took Corporations or Income Taxation does not distinguish you from any other candidates.

Revise your prior job descriptions.

I've never seen your resume. Yet, I know what it says about your prior work experience as a lawyer or intern.

It has an agency, court, company, or law firm name, your title at the job, and then it has bullets or some paragraphs that all start with "Researched X" or "Wrote memo about Y," or "Negotiated and drafted contracts on Z," or "Took deposition of Mr. T," or maybe if you're a badass, "Argued motion in federal court about S."

What's wrong with that?

No one cares what specific substantive things you did at your prior legal internships and jobs!

You're almost never going to get hired with less than five years of experience because of the specific substantive things you did at a firm, government internship, etc.

Lawyers know what young lawyers do. You don't have to tell them unless it is unique and applicable.

Instead, I recommend something like the following (which is the job description I used for my first law firm job after law school):

Greenebaum Doll & McDonald PLLC, Lexington, KY
Environmental/Mergers & Acquisitions Attorney, August 2004—August 2005; Summer Associate, 2003
- Large corporate law firm with highest-ranked environmental practice group in Kentucky;
- Represented electric utilities, coal companies, manufacturing facilities, city, state, and local governments, and various other industries;

- Worked with a partner in representing a coal company in its sale of $60 million dollars in assets; then handled numerous smaller $500,000-$7,000,000 asset sales on my own for the same company;
- Evaluated as either exceptional or above-average by every partner with whom I worked;
- Annualized at 1,900 hours when I voluntarily left the firm to pursue an LL.M degree.

I'm not saying this job description is perfect. Far from it. I wrote it as a young lawyer; today I would likely write it differently.

Still, let me walk you through why I think this was a persuasive, effective job description that helped me land a few jobs.

Since I was one of those nerds who loved civil procedure in law school, it's only fitting that I do so via some rules.

Job Description Rule 1: Start by describing your previous employer in glowing terms.

Right under the firm name and position, I used my first bullet point to tell you about my place of employment. I made sure you knew that my firm and practice group were big deals in Kentucky.

Why did I do that? <u>Selling the firm sold me.</u>

You should do this even if everyone in the world knows about the company or law firm you worked for. If you interned at Google, for example, in the first bullet point you should still tout how many lawyers were in your group or that you worked for the top Google privacy lawyer. If you were a summer associate at DLA Piper, on the other hand, you should tout the groups or subgroups you did work for or the specific partners who you worked most closely with.

And obviously if there's any chance that the reader might not recognize the name of the law firm or government agency or company, tell them about what makes it cool or different.

Doing these things ensures that the reader knows both where you worked and knows why the place you worked is impressive.

Job Description Rule 2: Never just describe prior day to day job responsibilities.

In my job description, I did not tell you about pleadings I drafted or memos I wrote. I never said what types of issues I researched. Or that I got to work on high-profile cases.

Instead, I tried to come up with something more interesting and pertinent to employers that might distinguish me.

My second bullet, for example, listed the kinds of clients I worked for. This showed, hopefully, that I understood that the clients are the business. And I had experience working with, and didn't have any problem working for, lots of different types of clients.

Then in the third bullet I told them about one large, noteworthy project:

- "Worked with a partner in representing a coal company in its sale of $60 million dollars in assets; then handled numerous smaller $500,000-$7,000,000 asset sales on my own for the same company;"

Why this one project? Because what happened shows that I gained both the clients' and the partner's trust; they handed over responsibility to me on subsequent deals.

Now go back and look at your own prior experience section. If a supervisor let you run a case, say so. Or if a client asked for you by name after working with you as a summer associate, say that. Or if you won something in court, say that.

Job Description Rule 3: Always, always, always tell them you got excellent reviews from your previous employers.

Unless you didn't. Then ignore this rule.

If you worked somewhere, they reviewed you, and they liked you, then hell fucking yes you put that on your resume. <u>That's what your future employers want to know.</u> They want to know that the people you worked for liked you.

This is literally the most important piece of information you can provide for any prior job description. (This is also why you should keep every written review an employer gives you, so you can show those reviews to your future employers later if you need to.)

Job Description Rule 4: Explain why you moved on.

Unless you got fired.

"Why did she leave?" is a question no one should ever have to ask when looking at your resume.

I decided to leave Greenebaum, Doll & McDonald to get an LL.M degree, so I said so on my resume. You should do the same. Maybe it's: "Voluntarily left position to relocate to be closer to my wife's family in Texas." Or: "Decided to pursue my dream of becoming a trial lawyer." It doesn't matter.

Your resume should be a guide that foresees, and then answers, questions. Your resume should never, for any reason whatsoever, leave open the possibility that you might have gotten fired or were asked to resign at a previous position.

If you don't say why you left, the reader will assume the worst. If you don't say why you didn't get a job offer after your summer internship, people will wonder about it.

Of course, if you were fired or asked to leave, don't say that on your resume. (But you do have to own it if someone asks you about it, and be sure to have an honest conversation about why that position didn't work out for you and your past employer.)

Job Description Rule 5: Never, and I mean never, list non-lawyer jobs on your resume unless they are particularly relevant to the job you are seeking.

No one cares what side-jobs you did in high school or college. No one wants to know much, if anything, about what you did between college and law school.

This should be obvious. But I've seen dozens of young lawyer resumes that make this mistake. Being a Sandwich Artist at Subway is not relevant to whether or not someone should hire you as a lawyer. Period.

The bottom line.

Remember, the very best types of resumes are the ones that tell a story—and hopefully, it's a professional story. You want to make sure that your job progression over time is clear and comprehensive.

If you can, you should also use your resume as a space to make yourself look interesting. Remember, everyone has a skill. Everyone has knowledge—especially in the law field when you're competing against people who learned the exact same things you did in law school.

Use your resume as a place to really showcase who you are, what you bring to the table, and where you plan to go from here.

I like to travel, and I traveled quite a bit when I was younger. So, I made sure to say how many countries I've traveled to in my resume's interests section. I also had ping pong listed as a skill for many years—and no, I'm not kidding.

CHAPTER 11:
Your Writing Sample and Cover Letter Aren't that Good

It's OK. Mine weren't either when I was a young lawyer. (Yes, I went back and read them.)

Most young lawyers—even the ones who graduate with stellar grades from top law schools—can't write a brief or a motion if their lives depended on it.

The truth is that everyone thinks they are good at writing. Yet very few people are great writers. If you don't know if you're a great writer, you almost certainly are not.

Luckily, the people reviewing your writing sample and cover letter are likely to be more senior in the practice of law than you. And practicing law, for the most part, involves a ton of writing.

A fortiori, everyone who reviews your cover letter and writing sample is likely to be more experienced at writing than you.

They'll know it too. Which is good.

When a more senior lawyer reviews your writing sample, for example, they are likely to assume it won't be as good as something they would write.

That means all you need to do is present a decent cover letter and writing sample. Not perfect ones.

Before I help you create a decent cover letter and writing sample, however, my best advice is this: don't submit either of them if you can avoid it.

I'm serious.

When I'm part of the hiring process, I get a pile of application packets. I do a first cut based on resumes because it's the easiest way to cut down the pile. For most people, I'll never even look at their cover letter or, if I have one, their writing sample.

In other words, I usually only take the time to read an applicants' cover letter and writing sample IF I've decided the candidate is worth a deeper dive based on their resume.

Now, I'm sure a few people are going to email me after reading this book and swear that they always read every cover letter and writing sample submitted to them.

Good for you. Give yourselves a pat on the back.

I've done a lot of research on this topic, however. And I've found out that most lawyers are really busy, and they don't want to set aside the time to read a pile of cover letters from candidates they aren't interested in interviewing.

(OK, you got me. I didn't do a lot of research. But it makes sense.)

I use the cover letter and writing sample to see if a candidate can write. But I'm only going to take the time to read those things if I'm interested.

I don't have the time, or the desire, to read fifty cover letters and writing samples every time we hire someone.

From a practical perspective, that means I'm using the cover letter and, if I have one, the writing sample to cut candidates out of consideration, not to add them into consideration.

Here's how it usually works. Let's say you want to work in my group, and you send me just a resume with nothing else. It's possible you'll make it into my "I'm interested" pile and get a call for an initial interview without me ever looking at your cover letter or writing sample.

I'm a litigator whose practice depends on writing. Therefore, I eventually make every candidate send me a cover letter and writing sample before I weigh in on whether they should get an offer. But by then, you may have already had a chance to interact with me. Or to interact with another partner at my firm.

That gives you an advantage, even if your cover letter and writing sample suck, compared to the candidates who simply launched all of their materials at me on the front end and never got to interview with me in the first place.

Put simply, your cover letter and writing sample are more likely to hurt you than help you. That's why you shouldn't send them unless you have to.

Of course, you'll likely still need them at some point in your quest to find a job. A lot of firms and other jobs require one or both. You should therefore be prepared to put your best foot forward, if you can. That's where I can help.

How to write a cover letter.

I don't know about your law school career services office, but mine was very strict about the format and contents of the oft-hated cover letter.

"Keep your cover letter short and to less than a page," they directed.

"Don't repeat your resume in your cover letter," they advised.

"Always include a cover letter with every job application," they counseled.

And definitely "don't be too forward or cocky in what you say," they preached.

Being a naïve law student who did not know any better, I listened. In other words, my cover letters coming out of law school were boring and unmemorable.

Knowing what I know now, however, I recommend a much less rigid, much more case-specific approach. Think of your cover letter like your college essay. Tell them why they want you; why you are unique; and why you would be an amazing hire for them.

If you have a stellar resume and have a great chance of landing the job, then sure, be conservative with your cover letter. Don't take any chances. You don't need to.

But if your resume is weak compared to your competition, then be bold in your cover letter. Tell them the most interesting thing about yourself, regardless of its relevance. Taut your social skills. Taut your pole-vaulting prowess. Why not? It might be your only chance of getting their attention (assuming they even read it).

Bold and interesting is always better than vanilla and boring.

How do you be bold?

<u>Be confident!!!</u> (Those extra exclamation points are there to make you feel jazzed up!!!)

Of course, don't be crass like me. Or rude.

Tell them why you think you'd do an amazing job at the position. Tell them you'd be willing to do a project for them for free to prove your worth. Basically, be different and try to stand out.

If you're funny in writing, then say something funny. If you're a nerd, say so.

I'm a fan of using your first sentence to catch the reader's attention. Try to do that. If you're going to go bold, do it, or at least allude to it, in the first two sentences, which may be all that they read.

As for repeating what you have in your resume, obviously you shouldn't regurgitate everything in your resume. But highlighting your best attributes in both your resume and cover letter is fine.

As you should know by now, unless you were mindlessly dreaming about your next bath while reading the last chapter, your resume should have every pertinent selling point about you on it.

So, you'll probably have some overlap between your resume and cover letter. Unless you're a magician.

Last and certainly least, for cover letter length, I don't think it matters. Keep it pertinent. Don't let it run on. But if you have interesting things to say, and it takes more than a page, say them.

Pay attention to the job description when writing your cover letter.

For a moment, pretend that you're a partner at a high-profile law firm. You're looking for a new associate to bring onto your team. And you've convinced your group's managing partner of the hiring need.

What happens next?

Well, at every firm where I've been employed (four, in total), the hiring partners then take the time themselves to review and edit the job description that will be advertised. A few may be too busy to take the time to do it. A few partners might trust the recruiting department to handle it. Most of the time, however, the partners hiring the associates actually write the job posting themselves. (The firm's hiring or administrative folks then post the job listing on the firm's website and in other outlets.)

Why does this seemingly mundane detail matter? It means you should pay a lot of attention to what the job posting actually says when writing your cover letter.

Lawyers can usually say what they want in writing. You therefore must take each job posting at face value. Job postings are often intentionally specific about what is needed in a candidate. Yet, in my experience, candidates usually ignore them.

Of course, if a job description is a stretch for you, you should still apply. Apply, apply, apply! But if a candidate doesn't fit the job description and doesn't explain in their cover letter why he or she is applying, I'm going to hold that fact against them. I just am. I think most lawyers making hiring decisions will do the same. It shows that the candidate either did not pay enough attention to the job description or that they aren't being open and honest.

How to pick your writing sample.

At the end of the day, your writing sample really does need to represent your best work—even if it's not exactly the best thing since sliced bread.

You may only have a few options in your file folder. That's OK. Whichever one you pick is going to need work before you hand it over. As such, pick the most substantively interesting one, and go with it.

Giving them something substantively interesting to read is almost as important as giving them a well written writing sample.

Remember, you are asking people to read this thing.

If your writing sample is about a boring procedural issue, even if it's perfect, your reader is going to be asleep by page two. They also aren't going to love you for making them read it.

The form doesn't matter that much. A letter, memo, brief, or even an email is fine. Just make sure it's on a relatively interesting topic.

Also, don't submit a writing sample that someone else has obviously edited. I've seen people submit published law review articles; I've also seen people submit judicial opinions from their days as a clerk.

Don't do these things.

Many people will find these submissions unacceptable because they will know, or at least strongly suspect, that the sample isn't entirely your work.

In fact, if you really want to stand out: write a new writing sample, unassociated with law school or your prior jobs, on a topic of your choosing. Put a cover letter on it saying that you wrote this specifically for your job search because you thought it was an interesting topic and you wanted to ensure employers that the work was entirely your own. Your writing sample will definitely stand out if you do that, especially if it's good.

How to polish your writing sample.

First, the basics. Your writing sample should be less than 10 pages, double-spaced. The first three pages need to impress, because they are all that anyone will likely read.

You have to include a short cover page or blurb at the top letting people know what the sample is from, how you were involved in the project, and why you selected it as your writing sample.

<u>Always, always, always, solicit lots of opinions and feedback about your writing sample from impartial colleagues or friends who you trust to be honest with you.</u> A classmate, a friend, a professor, a legal writing tutor at your school, etc. Ask them to read your prized

piece and to tell you what they think. Then revise it again based on their feedback.

But before you even share your work with friends and family, you need to apply my five writing tips for dummies. Do them, and I guarantee your writing sample will improve.

My five writing tips for dummies.

I've written for *Forbes*, *The Wall Street Journal*, *Bloomberg*, and over a dozen other publications. I write briefs for money all day long.

Yet, as I've told you, I wasn't born with a pen in my hand. I was a dreadful writer in college. It wasn't until I began to seek help and looked at writing as an analytical exercise that I finally started to improve.

The best way I can describe it is that I went about improving my writing methodically. I met as much as I could with writing tutors my first year in law school. I read books about writing. And I learned some basic legal writing tips along the way.

These rules, and my systematic, over-zealous, and perhaps at times infatuated desire to perfect my writing allowed me to at least fake it, until I eventually made it.

Tip 1: Don't suck.

Legal writing is, for the most part, formulaic. Still, every lawyer has a slightly different writing style. Trying to write a cover letter or writing sample that appeals to every lawyer is therefore going to be difficult.

Luckily, for the reasons described above, your writing doesn't need to pop for everyone who reads it. What your writing does need to do, however, is obviously not suck.

That means your writing can't have spelling errors or typos. It can't have any grammatical errors. It has to cite to the law in the correct order of authorities (I've given this one a whole tip of its own!) And it can't obviously be wrong about the law.

That's it. Do those things and most people will not reject you because of your writing sample.

Tip 2: Everything written by you must be in an active voice.

If that tip didn't make you laugh or want to call me out as an idiot, then you need to work on identifying passive voice.

When I was a young attorney, I went to a legal writing lunch seminar. I learned a ton. But one thing stuck with me.

Our instructor gave us a list of words and phrases that are indicators of passive voice. Let me pass on his wisdom to you:

Cut out these words		
• by	• am	• has
• of the	• are	• will be
• to be	• was	• being
• is	• have been	• will have been

No really. Cut them out of the book (only if you have a hard copy; I'm not reimbursing you for your Kindle). Put them in your office. Tape them next to your phone.

While not all of these words always indicate passive voice, simply re-writing your work to not include them, if possible, is a relatively easy way to eliminate passive voice.

Go through your cover letter and writing sample. Go line-by-line. Eliminate as many of these words and phrases as possible and, at a minimum, you'll have enormously improved your legal writing.

I know, of course, that passive voice has a place in legal writing. It's just that place is so small and insignificant in the overall scheme of things that it's not even worth focusing time on, except maybe as a hobby.

So, just use active voice all the time (or at least try to).

Tip 3: Know the order of authorities.

If you're writing a brief to the United States Court of Appeals for the Seventh Circuit, you should, if at all possible, primarily cite to cases from the Seventh Circuit or the U.S. Supreme Court.

If you don't have authority from those sources, then cite to other federal circuit court decisions. Do not, however, cite a district court case from Texas and call the decision binding. Or Missouri. Or even Wisconsin, which is in the Seventh Circuit.

Of course, if you can only find district court cases that are relevant, it's fine to cite them. But you must understand that they do not bind the Seventh Circuit. What you say (i.e., the words you use in your writing sample) must also clearly recognize this.

Similarly, don't cite a federal or state regulation if there's a federal or state statute on point. Don't tell a court that an agency regulation binds it to some action. Federal and state statutes bind federal and state courts, respectively (unless the statutes are unconstitutional). Federal and state regulations do not.

Basically, every time you cite something in your writing sample, think about two things: (1) how does the authority you're citing relate to the other authorities that you are aware of and are discussing; and (2) is the authority you are citing binding on the decision maker.

Tip 4: Use short sentences.

Using short sentences is like using the active voice in legal writing. You can't go wrong keeping sentences short.

Yes, superb writing mixes shorter sentences with longer ones. But you don't need superb writing right now. *You just need to pass.* Eliminating long sentences will help you do that.

How short?

I mean very short. Use two words per sentence if you can. Use three if you must. At worst, use four.

I'm joking, of course. But try. Try hard. Just pay attention to it. Keep to less than ten words if you can. And a lot of people will think you're an incredible writer.

Tip 5: Use no more than four paragraphs between headings.

Has anyone ever told you that people's attention span in a meeting is 8 to 10 minutes? It is.

That means if a presenter wants to keep an audience's attention, she needs to do something new every ten minutes. Like sitting down after standing up for the first ten minutes. Or starting a PowerPoint or video after the first ten minutes. Or switching presenters every 10 minutes.

Headings are like switching presenters. They break things up for the reader. Forcing yourself to keep to less than four paragraphs between headings will force you to focus on the organization of your ideas and the structure of your arguments.

Does every one of my briefs adhere to the four-paragraph rule? Absolutely not. This book doesn't either. But if you adhere to the four-paragraph or less rule, your writing sample will improve. I'm certain of that.

* * *

Follow these five tips for your cover letter, writing sample, and everything you write for the rest of your life, and you'll do fine.

CHAPTER 12:
How to Find Job Postings Online

There is not now, and probably won't ever be, an all-encompassing online repository for legal job openings because lawyers are about as technologically savvy as a herd of cows.

I still know senior statesmen dictating notes for their assistants to type up. When asked, they think Facebook is a company that sells beauty products through the mail. Frankly, it wouldn't surprise me if some small law firms out there are still posting help wanted ads in their local newspapers.

The fact that lots of lawyers are technologically ignorant means you must plan your search for job postings accordingly.

This isn't to say that you should subscribe to the hard copy edition of the Topeka Tribune. It just means you might have to think outside the box when looking for help wanted postings.

Of course, search all the job posting websites that do exist, many of which are listed below. But—and this is important so wake up—<u>don't ever assume the online job repositories are comprehensive;</u> there are many other job opportunities lurking out there; you have to find those too.

Top job search websites.

I feel obligated to include a list of job websites in this book because every job-hunting book needs to have a list of the top job websites.

As such, below is a (very boring) list of some of the top job search websites for lawyers as of this handbook's publication:
- Indeed
- LawCrossing

- LawJobs
- CareerBuilder
- LinkedIn
- Monster
- USAJobs
- National Association for Law Placement (NALP)

Scour them. Scour your law school's job posting platform. Then, after you find some openings that interest you, apply, apply, apply.

Don't assume law firms use the top job search websites.

As stupid and time-consuming as it sounds, you must go to every law firm's job posting page to ensure you aren't missing anything. If you are limiting your search to five cities, search Google; find the top twenty to forty law firms in each city (more if you're searching in a big city); and bookmark their job posting pages. Then check back often.

This might sound like overkill. But once you set it up, checking everything weekly will take you ten or fifteen minutes. It'll be time well spent.

Don't miss out on your dream job because you weren't diligent enough to find it.

Federal and state court clerkship openings are easy to find.

The federal government consolidates all clerkship opportunities into a single website. Just go to OSCAR at https://www.oscar.uscourts.gov/.

OSCAR, or if I must spell it out for you—the Online System for Clerkship Application and Review—contains postings for all federal clerkships (chambers, pro se, death penalty, and bankruptcy appellate panel) and federal staff attorney positions. OSCAR is also a great place to research federal judge and staff attorney office hiring practices, preferences, and timelines.

As for state court clerkships, there's an equally handy place to find those. And there's a funny and random story about me finding the state court clerkship repository.

When I realized I needed to figure out how someone might go about finding state clerkship openings online, I went to Google, searched for "state court clerkships," and that took me to a few law school career services pages.

U.C. Berkeley law school's career service's page (where I got my LL.M) came up on the first page of the Google results. So, I clicked.

And that's where I found out that the law school where I got my J.D., Vermont Law School, has the best consolidated guide for state court clerkships.

(Is it telling that I had no idea my alma mater published such a guide? Maybe. But it is what it is.)

In fact, Vermont Law School has published the aptly titled, "Guide to State Court Judicial Clerkship Procedures" since 1994!!! (Exclamation points added for emphasis.) Numerous schools and law students rely on the helpful guide.

Don't forget about federal and state agency jobs.

In my nearly two decades of experience as an administrative lawyer, I haven't heard many people describe local, state, and federal government agencies as technologically savvy.

You should plan your online search for such job openings accordingly.

Some states have at least one consolidated job search website for state jobs. Find those sites. Search them.

Then don't assume that those websites include all open state agency positions. Because they probably don't.

I don't know how pervasive the issue is exactly. I didn't do a 50-state survey. But in some states, the state's consolidated job search website doesn't include positions from the other, non-executive branches of government (like the legislature).

The takeaway? You should take the time to figure out where all the agency job postings are in your states of interest.

To make it easier for you, below is a list of state agencies that often have in-house lawyers (obviously these differ by state). If you can't find a consolidated site, just find each agency website you're interested in and search all of them for job openings.

- Department of Justice/Attorney General's Office
- Department of Administration
- Department of Agriculture, Trade & Consumer Protection
- Department of Corrections
- Department of Commerce
- Department of Education
- Department of Health
- Department of Housing
- Department of Human Services
- Department of Labor
- Department of Military & Veteran Affairs
- Department of Natural Resources
- Department of Revenue
- Governor's Office
- Investment Board/Agency
- Office of Administrative Hearings
- Public Defender Office
- Public Utility Commission/Public Service Commission
- State Lottery
- State Colleges & Universities

Based on my conversations with numerous state-agency lawyers and mentees who've landed agency jobs, I can tell you that state agencies are wonderful places to start your career. They can provide upper-level experience early.

They can also lead to law firm and in-house jobs after a few years, if that's your goal. Agencies regulate businesses. Which is why businesses often like to hire former agency lawyers. As do law firms.

Of course, every agency job isn't going to lead to a law firm or in-house job. But some can. Be strategic and thoughtful about which agency you choose to target if you're looking to use the agency job as a stepping-stone in your career.

In-house and non-profit job openings can be difficult to find online.

While many such organizations will publish their openings on one of the top job search websites listed above, some will only post openings on their own websites. You should therefore search each organization's website for openings.

Basically, make a list of the top companies and non-profits you might like to work for and routinely check each institution's website for job openings. That's the only way to be certain you are finding all the open opportunities.

CHAPTER 13:
Things NOT to Do When Hunting for a Job

PANIC!

Maybe you're a 2L without a summer position in sight. Or a 3L without a job offer in hand. Or a recent graduate studying for the bar while also job hunting. Shit, maybe you're suddenly unemployed after twenty years at a firm. It doesn't matter.

If you're unemployed, there's one thing I know about you: you're scared shitless.

I've been there. You're sure you're a failure. You may have even looked in the mirror, in a moment of weakness, and yelled: "AHHH! I'm never going to get a JOB!!! AHHH!" in a whiney voice.

Stop it. That's not helping. In fact, it may be hurting.

Panicking can ruin your perspective and cloud your judgement. Plus, it's a proven biological fact that lawyers can smell fear.

Here's the truth: the vast majority of recent graduates who pass the bar and want to work end up employed. If you read this book while sober, and actually plan to do some of the things I recommend, it's highly likely you'll land a legal job of some sort within 6 to 12 months of being sworn in as a lawyer of the bar. How else do you think I can guarantee that you'll get a job, or I'll give you your money back? It's a numbers game.

You need to remember, however, that it can take a while to land your first job. About 35,000 law students hit the market at the same time every year. That's a lot of fresh blood. If you're coming from a lower-ranked law school, even with pretty good grades, it's hard to stand out in that crowd.

Fortunately, it gets easier and easier the further out from law school in your career you get. It turns out that real life presents a lot more opportunities, and differentiating factors, than law school.

Now, here's where a few of you say to yourselves that you aren't worried. You're tough. You've got this. You walked across nails to get where you are, and you're ready for anything.

Maybe that's true, and you're the exception. But I doubt it. Whether you admit it to yourself or not, you're worried like everyone else who's young and overly leveraged with loans and obligations is worried.

Some worry is a good thing. It means you care.

Just don't stress yourself out too much. Instead, start systematically attacking your job conundrum like you would any other problem in your life.

Not everyone graduates from law school with a job in hand. Almost no one graduates from law school with an offer in hand from their dream job.

You should therefore keep some perspective during your job search.

Be strategic and thoughtful about it. How long can you financially afford not to have a job? If it's a long time, then take your time.

If it's not a lot of time, then consider getting a filler, non-lawyer job to pay the bills. Wait tables. Bartend. Do construction. Drive an Über. Those things don't need to be on your resume because they aren't relevant to your legal career. They therefore will not "look bad" on your resume because they won't be on your resume at all.

Here's how I would strategize if I were currently unemployed. Let's say I have six months of runway to pay my mortgage, feed my family, etc. I'd cut that time in half: three months. And I'd make that my deadline for getting a job I actually want.

In other words, I'd go into that six-month period with a plan. If I don't have a job by three months in, then I'll start expanding my search to other cities, or government jobs, or whatever falls in my "other acceptable and more likely to land" jobs category.

Whatever you do, however, <u>do not</u> just …

Take the first job that comes around.

Why? Having a law job is better than not having a law job, right? WRONG!

Please, please, please don't just take the first job you get offered because you're scared you won't get another offer.

Taking the wrong job can screw up, or at least hugely hinder, your entire career trajectory. What's worse, you'll have to stay there for at least a full year. Twelve months is a long time—ask anyone who has been on COVID lockdown.

My rule of thumb, and I have some pretty good thumbs, is that you owe every new legal employer at least a one-year commitment for their investment in you. After a year, in my view, you owe them nothing. Nada. Zilch. After a year, do what is in your best interest in a respectable and nice way, and never look back.

It's the right thing to do to stay for at least a year. Plus, if you leave before the end of a year, people will question why. They'll ask at your next interview. And the interview after that. And after that. It could follow you for a while. To explain it, you'll have to either convince your interviewer that this job was so terrible you couldn't make it a full year. Or they'll assume you were fired.

Bottom line: don't jump at the first job, no matter how much you want to. A year or more of your life is a serious investment. Think it out. Talk to people about it. Listen to your friends, family, and colleagues, not your fears. Taking the first job that comes your way is not likely to make your resume more attractive or advance your career (unless you can be miserable and get great reviews).

Which brings us to our next thing you shouldn't do when job hunting. If you're less than five years out of law school, do not, under any circumstances…

Apply to paralegal or legal assistant positions.

Don't do it. No good can come of it.

This is not to say that there is anything wrong with being a paralegal or a legal assistant. Those are great, respectable, sometimes fun professions that pay pretty well.

But you are a lawyer. Not a paralegal. Not a legal assistant.

DON'T GIVE UP SO QUICKLY AFTER ALL THE WORK YOU'VE PUT IN TO GET THIS FAR!

And practically speaking, there are a ton of reasons why applying to these positions in your current place in life is a terrible idea.

First: it's a waste of your time to apply because they aren't going to hire you. Why would they hire a newly minted lawyer they know isn't going to stay? I guess you could try having a weird dance, where neither of you are honest with each other about your intentions.

But why?

Even in the very unlikely event that you do end up staying for more than a few months or even a year, they'll assume you'd never be happy with the job. They'd be right.

I mean, who wants to hire someone they know doesn't want the job? No one, that's who.

Don't kid yourself: having these jobs on your resume at this point in your career is not going to help you get a job as a lawyer. Paralegals do substantially different tasks than lawyers. As do legal assistants.

Regardless (and if you're still considering it at this point, I'm losing faith in you), if you end up deciding to go the paralegal or legal assistant route, you can do that later in your career. Do it after you've tried for years to get a lawyer job. Yes years. Possibly five or more.

At that point in your life and career, you'd know what being a lawyer (or at least trying to be a lawyer) is like. And the employers will take you seriously when you say you want to be a paralegal or legal assistant.

The bottom line is that you need to be patient and determined. Don't...

Give up.

It might take a few weeks, months, or even years. But if you keep looking, working, networking, and learning, you'll make it. Somehow. Some way. You'll make it. You'll find your way.

I don't believe for a second that anyone who makes it through the gauntlet that is law school, and then passes a bar exam, and then cares enough about their career to endure this handbook, can't make a decent living as a lawyer. If you keep putting forth the same effort that got you here, you will get to where you want to be.

CHAPTER 14:
Six People Interrogating You (A.K.A. the Interview)

Here you are. You submitted a thousand resumes, you finally got a call back, and now it's time to prepare for your interview. While the interviewing process is one of the most daunting processes that you'll ever experience in your professional life, the legwork that you put in to get to this stage is surely worth celebrating. You are getting very close to landing a job.

Now don't screw it up.

If you've made it to the interview stage, it means you were likely amongst the top-five candidates in the application pool. At this point, your resume and your writing sample have become irrelevant. They already like your skills; they've seen your experience; and they have a good idea of what you're capable of. Now, it's time to showcase your identity—and charm them.

They want to know who you are. In many cases, the interview is a popularity contest, nothing more. It's all about meshing and ensuring that you're making yourself stand out as a person first and as a lawyer second.

Find out who will be interviewing you.

If you don't know who will be interviewing you, it's important to find out before you show up. If you're interviewing with a three-person office, obviously you should just assume you'll be meeting with everyone. But if there is any doubt about who you will be meeting with, ask the recruiting person or whoever else you've been corresponding with to give you a list.

Literally, just email them or call them and say "I'd like to be as prepared as possible for my upcoming interview. Would you mind sending me the names of the people I'll be interviewing with so I can do some background research before I come in?"

Preparation is the key.

Once you have a list of names, it's time to get to work.

Research, research, research.

Research each of the people you'll interview with exhaustively. Learn about their beginnings, find out about where they went to school, read about their accomplishments, and give yourself some talking points and some potential questions to ask to make the interview feel more natural.

Here's the process I've used many times. First, I put each person's name on a separate sheet of paper, so I can create cliff-notes about each one. I then Google each person's name and find out as much as I can about them personally. Where are they from? Where did they go to undergrad and law school? What boards are they on? Etc.

I then search for their name on Westlaw or Lexis and try to find one or two recent cases they've worked on or articles they've written. I then read a decision from a recent case or two that they've been involved with and any recent articles I can find. When I'm finished with cliff notes about each person, I study them. I bring them with me to the interview. And I refer to them while I'm meeting with the person to refresh my memory.

Why do I do all of this?

Because it allows me to both feel prepared—and to actually be prepared—for the interview. I'll be able to talk to the person about something they might have an interest in. If I'm lucky, I might even be able to showcase my ability to talk about a legal issue or two. I also get to learn a little bit about the people who are deciding my future.

When I did this as a young lawyer, I assumed that all my competitors who were interviewing were being equally as diligent. After I started interviewing people as a third- or fourth-year associate at a law firm, however, I realized that a lot of people do not prepare ahead of time.

Many of the people I've interviewed might have read my bio ahead of time. But few have done more than that.

Do more! If you talk to them intelligently about a case they worked on, they are going to remember you. If you bond with them over where they went to school or what they like to do, they are going to remember you.

My favorite trick when I'm being interviewed is to reference a fact, not weirdly, about my interviewer that could not have come from their bio. You catch them by surprise. I've even had some ask: "How did you know that?"

I then explain that I researchd everyone I was interviewing with in depth before the interview. Not only does this answer ensure they aren't creeped out by my stalking, it also shows that I'm willing to go the extra mile.

Prepare a list of questions to ask during your interviews.

Here are a few I like to ask. These are mostly aimed towards law firms (where I have the most experience); many of them, however, are useful in all contexts.

Do you like working here? If so, why? (You'd be amazed at what people will tell you in an interview.)

How many hours did you bill last year? (I particularly like to ask law firm partners this question because if the partners are billing 2,000 hours a year, you know everyone below them is billing 2,500 or 3,000 hours.)

What legal issues are you working on right now? (This will give you an idea of what you would actually be working on if you got the job; and it gives you an opportunity to potentially showcase your ability to talk about and analyze legal issues.)

What clients do you do work for? (Again, this tells you who you would likely work for if you worked there.)

What's your favorite part of your job?

How are young lawyers mentored?

What do you like to do for fun? (If they say work, run away!)

What is the hiring decision process and when will a decision be made?

Obviously, you can also ask them for specifics about the job, the benefits, etc. too. And I usually like to end every interview with one last question: *Is there anything you'd like to know about me that we haven't covered already?*

I like to have about 20 to 25 questions prepared before going into an interview. That's usually enough to ensure that I never run out of things to talk about.

Quiz yourself in writing.

When preparing for an oral argument, I write down five questions I think I'll get from the court; and then I write out the answers to each question. I limit all answers to two or three sentences. I then say the answers out loud a few times and revise them until they sound right.

I also try to weave a theme or two into the answers. And I add a specific case cite, including a page number or other detailed fact, if I can.

I almost always get at least one of my five pre-prepared questions from the court. When I do, I'm ready.

You should use the same process for interviews. Write out five to ten questions you think you'll get. Craft the answers. Say them out loud. Revise them a lot. Word them how you want them to come across. Figure out ways to use the questions to present an interesting story about yourself. Or paint yourself in a good light.

Then say the final answers out loud a bunch of times. Act it out if you want.

Now, you're ready for the interrogations to begin.

The morning of... sucks.

Drink coffee. Lots of coffee. Eat a little. Not a lot. And be sure to get a full night's sleep the night before.

That's pretty much all I've got for you.

OK, maybe one more thing: show up twenty minutes early. Never be late.

How to make a good first impression.

First, look your best. Wear something professional that makes you feel good about yourself.

Second, smile and look people directly in the eyes for a few seconds *every time* you meet someone new. No exceptions. Make yourself do it. If your cheeks don't hurt at the end of a long day of interviews, you're doing it wrong.

Third, be confident and relaxed. Of course, this is easier said than done. But if you do the first two things (i.e., you look your best and smile), the third will be easier.

During every interview, show an interest in the job.

You'd think this would be obvious. But I've interviewed lots of candidates who did not seem interested in the position they were interviewing for.

Remember: the person is interviewing you, not the other way around. I don't care how qualified you think you are for the position. Do not, under any circumstances, make the person interviewing you try to sell you on the job.

You need to convince everyone you interview with both that you really want the job and that you are the best person for the job. To that end, make sure you tell every person you meet how excited you are about the possibility of working there. Be specific. Have a few pre-prepared reasons why you want to work there and point to those reasons in the interviews.

Doing the research I recommend ahead of time can also help show you're interested; certainly, if someone shows up in my office and has done a bunch of research on me, I'm going to assume they are interested in the job. Why else would they do that extra work?

Let them do the talking.

Which is easier said than done with some introverted lawyers. Yet, it's still a good rule of thumb.

How do you get them to talk?

Use your long list of questions! When you feel like you've been talking too much, or there's a lull in the conversation, ask one of them.

Tell them a story about yourself.

Stories are memorable. They endear you to people. There are lots of studies to back this up. If you tell someone where you went to school, what you studied, and where you worked, that's fine. They aren't likely to remember much of it. It's also not nearly as likely to make them like you, and remember you, as telling them a unique story about yourself.

So, try to sneak in a fun or cool story about yourself.

Your story doesn't have to be work related. In fact, it's better if it's not. Think about something funny and/or interesting (but not too racy or controversial) that has happened to you. Everyone has something. Make it personal. And don't brag. No one wants to hear about how you got the best score in your Constitutional Law class or won a moot court competition.

I once told a senior partner in a law firm about my recent encounter with Trey Anastasio, the lead singer of the band Phish, after seeing his Phish poster on the wall. We then swapped war stories. And he remembered me for it. Maybe that was a risky move in an interview. But I got the job.

Once you've landed on a story or two about yourself or something that happened to you, practice telling them a few times before you go to the interview. You don't want your story to sound rehearsed, of course. But the story should be something you are used to telling.

Tell it to some friends at the bar and gauge their reaction. Or tell your landlord or neighbor if you have kids and can't leave your apartment.

Keep it short (more than a minute but less than 5 minutes). Include as much detail as you can.

Telling a story humanizes you. It makes you unique. When you leave the interview, they may not remember your name. Or where you went to school. But they'll remember you as that person who had that funny or interesting thing happen to them. That will make them think of you fondly. Which is exactly what you want.

Close, close, close.

My father spent his entire career in sales. "In sales, you have to close," he'd always tell me as a kid. "Don't leave without getting the sale."

At the end of an interview, do the same thing. You're selling yourself. Make sure they're buying before you leave.

To be clear, I'm not encouraging you to demand employment before you exit the office. I am, however, encouraging you to make sure the interviewer has no qualms hiring you.

Try saying something like this at the end of your next interview:

"I've really enjoyed our conversation. Thanks for making the time! This job seems like a great fit. Do you have any concerns about me as a candidate that I might be able to address before I go? I'm an open book."

This turns the table. In my experience, if they have a concern, they'll ask about it. You then get the chance to address it (and hopefully it was on your list of questions you prepared before the interview and you were ready to answer their concern).

If they don't have any concerns, this question still helps you. They'll like the fact that you were confident enough to address any concerns they might have had.

Come up with your own way to close. I don't care how you do it. But always close the interview.

Then walk out like you own the place.

"Thank you" emails and cards are lame, but necessary.

Most people don't care if you send them. A lot of people won't even read them. But if one person reads your "thank you" email or card, and likes what you wrote, that could put you over the top when everyone you met with meets later to discuss you.

Therefore, as much as it pains me to say it: send them.

But be safe about it. Don't send thank you cards with a whiskey bottle on the front. Or with little bunnies on them. In fact, I think sending thank you emails is the safest route. But if you like sending cards, fine. Just be safe with the design and look of the card.

Most importantly, pay close attention to what you say in the thank you message. Be short, punchy, and upbeat with the message. Don't act desperate. No typos. No grammar mistakes.

Refer to something you talked about with the person, if you can. But it's not required. In short, write something nice. Write it well.

Interviewing no-no's.

I could fill a whole book with the mistakes I've been told about or personally seen people make while interviewing for a job. Shit, I've made a lot of them myself.

Here are a few of the biggest blunders you can make:

<u>Acting like you know an area of law, term of art, or other factual or legal issue when you don't.</u>

No one expects you to know everything. In fact, most people will assume young lawyers know less than they actually do. As such, if the person interviewing you starts talking about a tax case, and you don't know anything about tax law, say so. Don't try to fake it. If they catch you bullshitting, your chances of landing the job go to zero.

<u>Bragging about the other interviews you've been on or the other job offers you've received.</u>

If they ask you about other places you've been interviewing, obviously tell them. Don't lie. But it's risky to try to play up your value by pointing out that you are interviewing at a lot of other places or already have job offers elsewhere. Frankly, telling potential employers you have job offers elsewhere might make them think you won't accept the job, even if they offer it to you. Or it could make them wonder why you are interviewing at a firm in Chicago when their firm is in New York. Etc. etc. Basically, the risk of doing this is too high for the potential reward.

<u>Bad mouthing past employers or other potential employers.</u>

If you hated your prior summer associate position, try to avoid saying that (even if asked). In fact, try not to say anything bad about anyone during your interview. You likely do not know what the interviewer thinks about your prior workplace. Plus, when people really dislike a prior employer, that can raise red flags to a future employer.

<u>Regurgitating your resume.</u>

Lawyers are professionals. Most if not all of them will have looked at your resume before meeting with you. Or, if they haven't had time, they'll tell you that right at the beginning of the interview. Use your time in an interview to talk about something that you haven't written down for them already. Regurgitating your resume will not make you shine.

<u>Bringing up politics or religion.</u>

Unless you purposefully want to make your interviewer squirm and instantly start sweating, don't do it. Even if you think Bob Dole was the best politician of all time, and the partner you are interviewing with has a Bob Dole picture on her wall, don't bring it up. These are topics that are generally off-limits when interviewing. Raising off-limit topics will just make the person interviewing you uncomfortable.

<u>Being defensive.</u>

If you think people might view you as defensive on occasion, then you probably are. If you think you might have a habit of being defensive or appearing defensive, you should talk to friends and family about it. Figure out how to stop doing it. And don't do it in an interview. Making an excuse or two is fine, of course. It's all in the delivery. If you failed the bar, and they ask you about it, own it. Then give an impartial, non-defensive assessment of why you failed the bar without looking peaked.

<u>Admitting you're bad at writing.</u>

If you're in an interview and someone asks you whether you think you are a good writer, you say: "I like writing. I think I'm pretty good at it. But it's something I'm always working on and will always continue to put an emphasis on getting better at over the course of my career." No one expects you to be an amazing writer as a young lawyer. The key, and what every interviewer wants to see, is a willingness to listen to criticism, take it to heart, and try again.

CHAPTER 15:
What to Do When You Finally Land a Job

Take a bath in champagne! Go to the mall in your pajamas! Eat breakfast for dinner! Binge all of the *Star Wars* movies!

<u>Do whatever makes you the happiest.</u> You deserve it.

Landing a job is a difficult journey. Pat yourself on the back. Be proud. Even if it's not your dream job, that's OK. You'll have a long career; everyone needs to start somewhere.

After you've celebrated a bit, call your parents, call your friends, and reach out to all the people who've helped you along the way. Tell them you landed a job. Tell them how excited you are about it. Thank them for their part in it.

You might need these people's help again in the future. Stay in touch with them. Do nice things for them.

Next, it's time to do some quick housekeeping.

Follow-up with all the jobs you've applied to and haven't heard from, tell them you landed a job, and withdraw your application. Just because they might have ghosted you doesn't mean you should ghost them. Other readers of this book might need those jobs. They shouldn't have to wait in line behind you if you've already landed a job.

And that reminds me, even though you have a job now, you still need to think about your future. You'll need to keep all your networking channels open and expanding.

In other words, your networking agenda shouldn't change just because you landed a job.

Keep networking and meeting with new people. Never stop networking. Foster as many positive, enjoyable professional relationships as you can outside of work.

This book isn't about how to excel at your job. But you'll need to do that too.

In your new job, it's vital that you do your absolute best work, all the time. It's vital that you strive to get better at your work, all the time. It's vital that you be proud of your written work, all the time. And it's vital that you meet every internal and external deadline, all the time. (It's also vital that you take a lot of naps because doing all this stuff can be exhausting.)

If you want some more tips on how to succeed in your new job, read Chapter 21.

To summarize: Write well. Impress them. Befriend them. Network with them. And, ultimately, make sure that if you later decide to leave your job, you can get top-notch recommendations from them.

Getting above-average reviews is your ticket to moving up.

Which brings me to something else you're probably going to need to know how to do to end up in your dream job: you need to know how to leave your current job for a better one.

CHAPTER 16:
Jumping Ship

Even if you love your current job, the odds are good that you'll move around a lot in your career. I did. I worked at four different law firms before turning forty. That forced me to learn how to effectively switch jobs.

In the end, it was painful and stressful. But I made it through without burning any bridges by being honest and open with all parties involved. In fact, I still have pretty good relationships with all of my former colleagues. (At least I think I do.)

The formula for switching jobs effectively.

While you might not believe it, there actually is a well-documented formula to help you switch legal jobs effectively—and guess what? It's all right here in this chapter.

I've turned switching jobs into a science, and it's one that you can learn quickly.

You see, it all begins with a few simple actions that revolve around respect, professionalism, honesty, and persistence.

Let's say you've interviewed for another job and received a written offer. You really want to take the new job.

What do you do next?

Do you:

(A) Put in your two-week notice.

(B) Quit on the spot and walk out the door.

(C) Go to your current employer and tell them you have an offer that you are considering taking.

The answer is always (C). Even if you have no interest in staying at your current job. Even if you hate everyone you work with, and they hate you too. It doesn't matter.

Always tell your current employer you got an offer you are considering, let them talk to you about it (and maybe even offer to fix things or up your salary), give it a few days, and then if you still want to leave, tell them that.

Pro-tip: do not go to your current employer with your new job offer until all contingencies on your new offer, such as conflicts, have been cleared.

It's critical as part of this process that you inform your current employer why you are considering the new offer, and why you think it might be a better opportunity to help you advance your professional career. Talk to them about the new offer, be open, be respectful, be honest, and be persistent. At the end of the day, when you successfully navigate a job switch, there's really nothing that they can hold against you.

Often when you tell your employer that you have another job offer, they will make a counteroffer. If they really don't want to lose you, they might consider a promotion, a raise, or a title change—all of which would be wonderful for you.

If you stay at your existing job because they offered you a raise, promotion, and/or pledged to make working more pleasant, however, don't go shopping for other jobs again anytime soon. If you go back to them again within a year or two with a different job offer, you're bound to get a much different reception. You might even end up getting escorted to the door.

On the other hand, you might run into a much different reception when you tell your existing employer about your new job opportunity. They might want you to go. They might not make you a counteroffer. Which will leave you in the position to choose the only, and likely the correct, path for you.

Take as much time off as you can between jobs.

The three weeks off between my second and third firms were not only an amazing time in my life, but they were my new boss's idea.

There was no pressure to do anything during those blissful weeks. Nothing. I was unemployed with a job.

I still remember the conversation with my soon-to-be-new boss. Doug (the partner) flat out told me over the phone to take two months off if I could afford it. I had just asked him when he wanted me to start. He said something like: "Don't worry. We're not too busy. But we have plenty of work for you when you get here. This is a big firm; others can cover for you for as long as you need."

He knew that once I started, I'd only be able to take a few weeks off a year. And he had taken some time off between jobs before, which he described as the best time of his life.

He was right.

One rule to live by.

There's something that I truly believe is a strong principle to hold on to when it comes to switching jobs. You too should follow this rule: Never stay in your current job because you're worried about what your colleagues, partners, or current bosses might say if you leave.

For many of us, our career means a lot—we use it as a sense of pride, and we cherish the relationships that we've built with our co-workers. Leaving behind a job that you loved for something bigger and better hurts—no matter what.

You simply can't, however, let that guilt or fear dictate your decisions. Anyone who truly considers themselves a friend of yours will be happy to see you succeed. They'll want to know all about your new position, and if it's located in a new city, they'll be the first people to come and visit you.

<u>You have to make career decisions for yourself, not your employer.</u>

Your career is going to matter a lot more than any of the work relationships that you build throughout your career. It might sound cold-hearted. But it isn't.

You have to look out for yourself. Which means you can't make career decisions based on how you think your co-workers, or your firm, might feel.

Anyone who you consider a friend should be happy for you if you leave for a better professional opportunity. If they act hurt or are mad at you for leaving them behind, they aren't your friends.

CHAPTER 17:
Understand the Business of Law

Law schools should teach students the business of law. Yet most don't. They teach you how to do research; how to read cases; and if you're lucky, how to write effective briefs and memos. Which is all fine and good.

When you get out into the real world of lawyering, however, what you also need to know is how the lawyering business works.

You have to understand your own business. Right now, you're probably clueless. But I can help. Let's start with the basics.

Lawyers are consultants.

Ever hire a plumber? Or an architect? Or a painter?

When you hire one of those folks, what do you care about?

You care about them doing a good job and being efficient.

Practicing law is the same. Whether you are in private practice and your clients are Fortune 100 companies; you work in-house and your clients are the company's business executives and shareholders; or you work in a government lawyer job and your clients are agency officials: all clients want the same thing.

They want useful answers created as efficiently as possible.

Never forget those two goals whenever you are practicing law: good work, efficiently completed.

Now, as a young attorney one of those goals matters much more than the other. Can you guess which one it is? (HINT: it's not efficiency.)

Good work matters more than anything when you are a young lawyer. Why? Because as a young lawyer, everyone will expect you to be inefficient. That's why first-year associates have the lowest billing rates in law firms. Your time as a young lawyer is cheap. And, even if you are working somewhere that does not bill by the hour, you will be the lowest on the totem pole.

No partner or supervisor wants you to send them a draft of something you did quickly. They want you to send them something that makes their life easier and allows them to work less.

Efficiency is something that you will get better at. <u>But never trade efficiency for quality in the first five or ten years of your legal career.</u>

Time is money.

I'm not talking about your time. I'm talking about everyone else's time. This is especially true if you work at a firm where billing by the hour is still the norm. While alternative fee arrangements, like flat fee and monthly retainers, are getting more popular, they are still used less than the good old billable hour.

Generally speaking, a first-year associate will have a lower hourly rate than a mid-level associate. A mid-level associate will have a lower hourly rate than a junior partner. And a senior partner will have the highest rate. Conversely, paralegals generally have lower hourly rates than a first-year associate. As do assistants (if the firm bills for their time at all).

You probably already knew all of that. Fine. But take it to heart and think about it from an efficiency standpoint. That's how the client and most partners will look at it.

If your assistant or a paralegal can do something to make you get your assignment done more efficiently, you should ask him, her or they for help. Similarly, if you can ask a mid-level associate to answer your question rather than the partner, you should ask the cheaper mid-level associate.

Always consider efficiency with everything you do as a young attorney. Always.

Basic lawyer math.

Many young lawyers think it's crazy how much money is charged for their time. To be clear, it's obscene.

But you also need to think about some of the practical ramifications associated with charging by the hour.

If a lawyer charges $250 per hour, they will need to bill 2,000 hours a year to generate $500,000 in revenue.

If a lawyer charges $500 per hour, on the other hand, they can bill half as much time to generate the same $500,000 in revenue. Or they can bill 2,000 hours at $500 per hour and bring in twice as much money.

It sounds simple but lots of lawyers forget this simple fact. It's easier to attract work when you charge a lower rate. But if you can charge a higher rate, you can make more money, and you will have more time.

Put simply, whether you want more money OR you want more time, the higher rate is the way to go (assuming you can pull off a higher rate).

Of course, this assumes you can choose your hourly rate. But, actually, as a law student or young attorney, sometimes you can do just that.

Certain areas of the law demand higher rates (e.g., Corporate, Tax, & IP litigation). So, if you are considering whether to become an employment lawyer or a corporate lawyer, you might want to consider that employment lawyers often have lower rates. Similarly, certain firms have higher rates than other firms (e.g., AmLaw 100 v. 200).

The bottom line is that when you're starting out, you might actually have some say over your rate trajectory. Consider rates early on in your career. You could end up saving yourself time and making more money in the future by doing so.

Know your clients.

Like with rates, which clients you end up working for can have a huge impact on your personal and professional life. If you work for large corporate clients, they're likely to pay higher rates. They're also likely to have lots and lots of work.

When I was first starting out, I quickly learned that geography can also impact who your clients are. After graduation, I headed home to Kentucky to practice environmental law. It never dawned on me when I made this decision that the type of clients and legal issues I would face at a law firm in Kentucky doing environmental law might be substantially different than those I would face if I had decided to practice environmental law in Vermont, Washington D.C., or California, for example.

Coal is king in Kentucky. Many of my projects therefore involved representing companies mining for coal or companies burning coal.

Conversely, when I relocated to Wisconsin a few years later, I ended up doing a lot of ethanol and other biofuel work. (Wisconsin has a lot of corn and soybeans, which are used to make biofuels.) Most of my career since then has focused on renewable energy because Wisconsin adjoins Iowa and Minnesota, which have some of the best wind resources in the world.

You should think about these things <u>before</u> deciding where to search for jobs. If you are interviewing for a firm job, ask them who their main clients are and figure out what types of issues those clients might have in your field. You might just find out that they do work you don't want to do, or vice versa.

Ensure clients pay bills.

This advice isn't necessarily relevant to the job hunt.

It is, however, relevant to you getting an offer if you're a summer associate. And it's relevant to staying employed if you're already employed. It's also relevant if you decide to sell your services as a lawyer to a client (which, for some reason, seems like it might be pertinent for most of you).

Here's the bottom line. So much time and money are lost due to lawyers, particularly young lawyers, not understanding how to document their time in a way that clients will pay for.

The strategy I use is fairly simple.

Every time entry you write should start with one of these five words: *Research, Draft, Edit, Analyze*, and possibly, if you feel so obliged, *Consult*.

Don't ever write a time entry that doesn't start with one of those words.

That's it. Lesson complete.

Let me give you some real life-like examples:

> Here is a time entry a client will always pay for:
> *Research and analyze whether Jim Smith has a viable takings claim; draft email to* [insert partner name according to billing nomenclature] *summarizing results of research*
>
> Here is a time entry that the partner will have to re-write:
> *Read John v. Doe, read Adams v. Smith, call T. Jones to discuss possible claims, write email to partner*
>
> Here is a time entry a client will always pay for:
> *Analyze documents to be produced for attorney/client information; redact same*
>
> Here is a time entry that will really piss the partner off (particularly if it gets through their filter to the client):
> *Review documents*

You get it. Be short. Be descriptive enough. But don't be too descriptive.

Never assume the reader of your bill has any idea what you were working on. It could be 30 to 90 days before anyone looks at your time entry to decide whether to pay it.

Basically, look at your time entries and think to yourself: would

I pay for that assuming I knew nothing about this matter? If the answer is no, re-write it using one of the five words.

Remember, if you're at a firm, your time entries might be the only thing you write for a while that a client actually sees.

CHAPTER 18:
To Specialize or Not to Specialize?

When I was in law school, I was told to specialize in a particular area of environmental law. Doing so would make me stand out and be more marketable, was the direction I was given.

I'm not sure what law students are being told now. But whether or not to specialize, and if so, in which particular legal field, are difficult questions to answer. Especially in a book. Details matter.

Still, I've got some thoughts and a lot of numbers to throw at you.

Do what makes you happy.

This should hopefully be obvious.

If you love animal law, and it'll fulfill your life's dream to work in-house for PETA, then obviously go for it. Do your thing. You only live once.

But for those of you who aren't as tied to a particular area of the law, you may as well consider the current market for the different specializations you're interested in pursuing before deciding which area of the law to pursue.

Understand the current demand for the specialty you pick.

No one can guess the future. I focused on the Clean Air Act in law school, which is about as esoteric a specialty as one can possibly pick. Then I got lucky. About five years out of law school, the Clean Air Act became a hot area (partly, but not completely, because of greenhouse gas regulation). I was suddenly incredibly well-versed in an area that a lot of other lawyers did not know well.

My successful choice of a specialty was blind luck. You shouldn't follow my lead and hope to get so lucky.

If you aren't in love with any particular specialty, why not do some research about how many jobs are likely to be in each area before picking?

When a law student tells me that they want to specialize in patent litigation, for example, I always tell them that patent litigation as a nationwide practice is down. Therefore, there may not be as many patent-litigation jobs available as compared to other litigation specialties. That doesn't necessarily mean that this person shouldn't try to follow their dreams. It just means they should go in with their eyes open, knowing it's a risk.

For those of you who are too lazy to do the research yourself, here are some hot specialties as of 2020:

Hot Specialties	*According to...*
Elder Law	*Attorney At Law Magazine*
Healthcare Law	*Attorney At Law Magazine*
Labor and Employment Law	*Attorney At Law Magazine; National Jurist*
Privacy and Cybersecurity Law	*Attorney At Law Magazine*
Bankruptcy Law	*Attorney At Law Magazine*
Commercial Litigation	*National Jurist*
Insurance Defense	*National Jurist*

Bottom line: don't just trust this list. Google search "hot specialties," "top lawyer specialties," or "highest growth areas" and law. Read what you find, and gut check whether you believe it.

If money matters to you, read this section.

The Bureau of Labor Statistics publishes tons of lawyer salary data online every year. According to BLS's 2020 data, for example, here are the average mean salaries for some popular legal occupations:

Legal Occupation	**Average Salary**
All Lawyers	$153,490
Privately Owned Firm Lawyers	$157,230
Federal Government Lawyers	$145,010
State Government Lawyers	$106,440
Securities Lawyers	$201,630
Real Estate Lawyers	$176,150
Elder Law Lawyers	$74,720
Non-Profit Lawyers	$113,250
Social Assistance Lawyers	$83,680

I'm not providing these numbers so that you necessarily pick the highest-paid specialty or career path (although feel free if that's your thing).

Instead, the point is that these salary numbers (and more than 250 additional lawyer job category numbers) are publicly available. If money matters to you, take a look at the salary data before picking your specialty.

Remember, however, that the BLS's salary numbers include all lawyers, regardless of seniority. Newer lawyer salaries, on average, are obviously less.

In-house counsel jobs, for example, start-out at an average salary of $91,750, according to the *Robert Half 2019 Legal Salary Guide*. And the same publication says the average first-year associate at a law firm makes $70,500. (Biglaw starts out at $190,000.)

Regardless, the BLS summary data should give you a good indication of the relative salaries between different lawyer job-types, which can help inform your career and educational choices.

CHAPTER 19:
Advice for Foreign-Trained Lawyers

Author's Note: In case the title isn't obvious enough for you, this chapter is only for foreign-trained lawyers.

I live in Madison, Wisconsin. I was born in Boston, Massachusetts. And I was raised in rural Kentucky.

Maybe some people who live in New York City or Los Angeles think Kentucky is another country and would consider me to be a foreign national. I certainly don't. Nor am I a foreign-trained lawyer, an immigration lawyer, or even an international lawyer.

I therefore can't give foreign-trained lawyers any advice based on my own personal experiences. And people with real world experiences, in my view, give the best advice. (If you want free mentorship from a real foreign-trained U.S. lawyer, just email me, and I'll connect you to one.)

I do, however, have a lot of experience talking to, and mentoring, foreign nationals looking for legal jobs in the U.S. In fact, I've spoken to and mentored well over a hundred such lawyers—just during the time I've been writing this book. Plus, back in 2006, I obtained my LL.M in a class full of foreign-trained lawyers, dozens of whom were simultaneously looking for jobs in the U.S.

In other words, although I'm an outsider, I've learned a lot from these experiences. So, I thought I'd share some insights and (hopefully) impartial observations.

Before we delve into any specifics, however, let's make sure you have the requisite background from a real professional in the area: my good friend Professor Erin M. Barbato, Director of the Immigration Justice Clinic at the University of Wisconsin Law School.

Requirements for practicing law in the U.S. (By Professor Erin M. Barbato).

Foreign nationals seeking law degrees in the United States should plan their educational and career journeys carefully. There are many countries in the world where law degrees are the equivalent of an undergraduate degree in the United States.

To become a licensed attorney in the United States, however, a foreign national will need to not only earn a professional level or master's level degree, but also pass a bar exam, and obtain an employment-based visa to work lawfully.

This is a complicated process. If the foreign national desires to practice law in the United States, they will need to know the type of law degree needed, the specific rules of the jurisdiction where they wish to practice, and most likely have an employer sponsor them for an employment-based visa.

Not all law degrees in the United States are equal. It is important that foreign nationals seeking law degrees in the United States understand the benefits and requirements of each degree. Certain degrees will allow foreign nationals to eventually practice law in the United States, while others will not. Each law school should provide information to prospective students to ensure they are aware of the parameters of each degree.

Many law schools offer academic programs leading to Juris Doctorates (J.D.), Masters in Law (LL.M), or Doctors of Juridical Science (S.J.D). Not all law schools offer all three, however.

The most common degree, a J.D., follows the traditional three-year academic program. This is arguably the most intensive program, with the highest standards for admission. If a foreign national earns a J.D., they will need to also take a bar exam to become a licensed attorney. If the student passes the bar exam, then the foreign national can practice law in the United States.

A second option for foreign nationals is an LL.M, which is also called a Master's in Law degree. The LL.M allows foreign nationals that have law degrees from another country to study law in the United States. This degree is normally a two-semester program.

An LL.M. may permit the foreign national to sit for the bar examination in certain states. For example, California, New York, Illinois, and Wisconsin allow foreign nationals with LL.Ms to sit for the bar exam. This program does not require an LSAT score for admission, which is often attractive to foreign nationals with law degrees from other countries.

The third option for a law degree is a Doctor of Juridical Science (which are commonly referred to as a S.J.D. or J.S.D.). This is a research-based law degree program that some foreign nationals pursue if they have a J.D. or LL.M from an American law school, or an equivalent degree from a university outside of the United States. These programs vary in length, lasting up to four years. This may be a route for a foreign national to pursue a career in academia but is not typically pursued for those wanting to be a licensed attorney.

During law school, foreign nationals are usually required to have a valid F-1 visa. This is a non-immigrant visa status that must be maintained during the pendency of the law degree program.

After law school, things get trickier. One of the largest barriers for foreign nationals to work as attorneys in the United States is obtaining an employment-based visa to work after graduation and passing a bar exam. <u>A job offer from an employer does not permit a foreign national to work in the United States.</u>

As a student, the foreign national is normally in F-1 status, which does not allow work outside of the academic institution. An employer seeking to hire the foreign national will often apply for an H1-B to employ the foreign national. Certain foreign nationals may have a year in OPT (Optional Practical Training) while they wait for an H1-B. The H-1B has a lottery system which leaves many people who qualify and apply without a visa in the end.

The employer and foreign national will want to seek counsel from an immigration attorney who specializes in employment-based visas, as it is a complex area of law that is frequently changing. If the foreign national has another way of seeking lawful status through family or even through a humanitarian-based route such as asylum, these options should also be explored as well.

My tips for foreign-trained lawyers.

As Professor Barbato just so eloquently outlined, foreign nationals need to jump over numerous hurdles before they can work as a lawyer in the U.S. They need to get into a U.S. based law degree program; they need to complete that program; they need to pass a bar exam; and they need to find a job. Moreover, even if they do all those things, they're still not guaranteed to get an H1-B visa (because it's a lottery system). So, even if things go swimmingly for you, you could end up getting a degree, passing the bar, and landing a job, yet still not be able to stay in the U.S. merely due to bad luck.

I've seen this happen to my mentees. It's not rare.

I can't help you win the lottery. If I could, I'd have retired by now. But I do have some general job tips for foreign-trained lawyers looking to work in the U.S.

Here they are, in no particular order.

You'll be judged on your writing more than other applicants.

I only speak one language fluently. It therefore blows my mind that people can learn English as a second (or even third or fourth) language, go to a law school taught in English, and then pass a bar examination in English.

I'm not alone. American lawyers aren't the most lingual bunch. Indeed, most attorneys in the U.S. only speak one language.

And there are tons of American-born, native English-speaking lawyers who don't write well. Fair or not, some potential employers will therefore implicitly, or even explicitly, assume someone who speaks English as a second language won't be as good at legal writing as other, native-English speakers.

What does this mean for you if you're a foreign-trained lawyer looking to get hired in the U.S.?

It means you will be judged more critically on your writing than your U.S.-trained J.D. counterparts. Plan accordingly.

If you're still in your home country and planning to come over to the U.S. for an LL.M, for example, focus on your English writing skills. If you just started your LL.M program, go see writing tutors. Even if you've landed your first U.S. job already, for at least the initial few years of your career, you're going to be judged differently. Be cognizant of that fact.

And…

Don't make mistakes.

It really comes down to careful and thoughtful reading and writing. Read every email you send closely. Print it out. Read it. Revise it. Print it out again. Read it. Revise it again. Make sure that you fully understand and comprehend what someone is saying to you in an email, and then be sure to review your own response many times, from many angles.

Don't take grammatical risks. Always try to keep your sentences short and to the point. The less said in email, the better—especially if you feel as though you can communicate more effectively in person than through writing.

Moreover, at the very least, always try to have someone else look over your writing to make sure that proper syntax, punctuation, and grammar are maintained throughout. You want to give yourself every chance to succeed, and by addressing your potential shortcomings, you'll be one step ahead of the rest of the competition—and there will be a lot of it.

Make sure people understand how talented you are.

If you're an international lawyer pursuing or already practicing law in the U.S., you're a talented person. I'm certain of it. You've mastered a difficult profession in two countries; probably done one of them in a second language; and passed legal entrance exams in two countries.

Don't let anyone looking at your credentials forget these facts. You must tout your accomplishments in your home country in a way American lawyers can understand. Make sure your resume does that. Paint a picture. Say that the bar passage rate in Japan was 39% the year you took it, for example. Tell the reader how challenging it was for you to get hired into, and then excel at, your financial crimes job in Shanghai before you decided to voluntarily leave it to come to the U.S.

Try to turn your differences with other non-international candidates into positives. But…

Keep your expectations realistic.

Most foreign-trained lawyers are studying for an LL.M degree when they start looking for their first jobs. Some may go through the J.D. program first. But most just try to get an LL.M.

As a foreign-trained lawyer, earning a job in the U.S. with just an LL.M is a difficult task—but that doesn't mean it's impossible. You'll need to have a little bit of luck on your side, but you'll also need to be strategic in the ways in which you present yourself.

Always make sure that your expectations are realistic. Far too often, foreign-trained lawyers think that the only barrier to entry into the U.S. market is an LL.M degree. As such, they'll apply to a bunch of LL.M programs, study hard, get an LL.M degree, and then start applying for jobs after passing the bar (or while studying for it) only to realize that the market is extremely competitive.

If only it were that simple.

Instead, you should assume that getting hired as a foreign-trained lawyer with only an LL.M degree is going to be hard. You should follow the advice in this book about building your network. Choose five U.S. cities that you are willing to work in. Get out there. Meet people. See the world. Connect with firms. Work for free for a few months if you have to—whatever you can do to make sure that you stand out from the crowd, the better.

You see, these tips are simply my way of helping you ensure that you can get out there and succeed as a lawyer. It isn't easy. I wish I had help when I was first starting out. But I didn't. Don't be like me. Instead, take advantage of the information that I'm sharing with you and give yourself every opportunity to achieve success.

CHAPTER 20:
The LL.M Conundrum

Author's Note: This chapter is for everyone considering getting an LL.M degree.

For those of you who have an LL.M degree or are currently attending an LL.M program, you probably know what conundrum I'm talking about. You already went through it.

The conundrum is whether or not to pursue an LL.M degree.

These degrees are not cheap. Mine added $50K in loans to my already hefty loan total. And it's unclear whether the benefits of getting an LL.M degree are worth the cost. Some law professors have even dubbed them "Lawyers Losing Money" degrees.

This chapter will help you decide whether an LL.M is right for you.

But first, if you're thinking about getting an LL.M, let's start with the basics.

What are LL.M's for?

As described in the last chapter, LL.Ms are predominantly for foreign nationals who want to practice law in the United States. If a person has a law degree from another country, and they want to practice law in the U.S., they can get an LL.M degree and practice law in many U.S. states. They don't need a J.D. to do so.

In my LL.M class, there were about 55 students. Less than five were Americans. The rest came from over 25 different countries.

Many LL.M students have been practicing law in another country for years before coming to America. They have a lot of practical experience. They are serious students.

Some want to stay and practice law in the U.S. Others want to go home with their U.S. law degree because it will up their market value in their home country. Some want to teach law internationally (which sometimes requires an S.J.D. or J.S.D.).

For schools and institutions, LL.M programs are major money makers. LL.Ms typically take about one school year to complete, but you can learn an awful lot about the American legal system in a school year. In addition, they're often not graded on the J.D. curve, so that means that you can focus more on your studies and job search and less on your GPA.

Who should consider getting an LL.M degree?

Based on my own LL.M experience and talking to lots of LL.M students and graduates, there are exactly three situations when I think getting an LL.M degree makes sense:
1. If you have an international law degree and you want to practice law or at least be licensed in the United States.
2. If you want to teach law.
Or...
3. If you can't find a job or a job you like/want, you went to a law school that is not ranked in the top 14, and you can get into a top 14 LL.M program.

That's it. If you don't fall into one of those categories, in my (not so) humble opinion, the substantial financial cost of an LL.M degree isn't worth it.

I should know. I fell into both categories 2 and 3. I got my J.D. at a lower-ranked law school. After practicing a year at a mid-level regional law firm in Kentucky, I decided to apply to three top LL.M programs (I chose the highest ranked law schools in the "coolest" places, according to my 25-year-old self).

My logic in going down this path was as follows. My dream was to eventually become a tenured law professor. The odds of that happening with a law degree from Vermont Law School, however, were basically zero. I didn't go to a top 14 law school, and about 80% of tenure-track law professors have a J.D. from a top 14 law school. I didn't even go to a top 100 law school. I didn't graduate first or second in my class. My only chance, I thought, was going to a top LL.M program and publishing something in a top tier law journal.

That my partner and I also wanted to live in a different location at the time also helped spur my decision to apply. After spending our first year as lawyers in Lexington, Kentucky, we both knew that we did not want to spend our 20s living there. (It's a fine place, but 20-somethings were sparse.) Pursuing an LL.M degree gave me an out with a potential bump on my resume.

Looking back, I'd like to say I had some big grand scheme at the time to work my way up to Biglaw by getting an LL.M degree first. I didn't.

At the time, I figured an LL.M from a top law school couldn't possibly hurt my resume. And I planned to spend my time in school writing as many law review articles as possible to prove myself.

Is an LL.M worth it?

It's hard to say.

Showing up on that first day of class and sitting next to a bunch of J.D. students was certainly a rude awakening. I couldn't help but question my decision.

Why was I back in law school classes with 2Ls and 3Ls? Why was I paying a ton of money to be in the same J.D. classes I had just left behind? It felt a little bit like going back to high school after finishing your freshman year of college. I totally freaked out for the first few weeks.

It took a while. But I eventually got over it and settled in.

I threw myself into studying and writing articles. Soon I realized that if I put forth even 75 to 80% of the effort I had put forth working as a first-year associate at a law firm, I could get a lot done. (It also meant I could use the additional 20 to 25% of my time gallivanting around Northern California's Bay Area.)

At the end of my LL.M year, I had written and published two law review articles. I got great grades (remember, LL.Ms aren't usually graded on the same scale as J.D. students). I also made some amazing friends.

But was my LL.M worth the financial investment? It's arguable.

Of course, it's basically impossible to measure whether my peers, colleagues, and clients over the years have ever cared that I have an LL.M degree. I've never had a potential employer raise it as a benefit. If anything, it raised more questions in the hiring process.

I also never tried to get hired as a law professor at the annual law professor meat market event (there's actually a single annual interview and hiring event). But I spent a lot of time researching the process, and concluded my chances were still very low, even with the LL.M. (Of course, I still applied to a few law professor jobs because, apply, apply, apply. But I never even got an interview.)

My LL.M also didn't help increase my salary. In fact, the opposite is true. I got paid less than other people in my class at my next two firms because the firms wouldn't give me credit for my LL.M year.

In all, I think I would have made it to the same place at the same time in my career had I never gotten my LL.M degree.

But I loved my LL.M year; I'm glad I did it; and I'd do it again even knowing what I know today.

OK, enough about me. Let's get back to you.

LL.M employment statistics.

Unlike J.D. employment statistics, LL.M employment numbers are much harder to find. That's because the ABA does not require law schools to disclose LL.M employment numbers.

The only LL.M programs I could find that disclose their employment numbers were tax LL.M programs, which likely have the highest employment rates.

Still, here's what I could find:
- N.Y.U. Tax LL.M: 95-97% employed within 10 months of graduation (2015-2018)
- Georgetown Tax LL.M: 94-99% employed within 10 months of graduation (2016-2018)
- Northwestern Tax LL.M: 94% employed within 10 months of graduation (2018)
- University of Florida Tax LL.M: 96% employed within 10 months of graduation (2019); however, 45% were employed at accounting firms.

Most other LL.M programs don't list their employment data, which means it probably isn't that compelling.

If you're considering an LL.M program, you should ask the school for its employment numbers. Most will give them to you. If they refuse, you should consider that to be a pretty big red flag.

If you already have a J.D., tread carefully.

Top 14 or bust!

If you already have a J.D., you obviously don't need an LL.M to practice law. You therefore need another reason to get one.

There are two common reasons given: teaching and specialization. However, only one of those reasons usually passes the smell test.

Quite a few people get LL.Ms for the sole reason of boosting their resumes in the teaching market. There is some anecdotal evidence that this works. But, obviously, the Ivy League faculty at a law school aren't going to be swayed by just any old LL.M. You'll need a degree from at least a top 14, and probably a top 5, program to help your chances.

Specialization is the other common reason I hear from those on the LL.M bandwagon. Most people who I have encountered who gave "specialization" as a reason for getting an LL.M, however, were covering up for the real reason: they just wanted a better school name on their resume.

I specialized in Energy Law for my LL.M. But really the specialization was secondary: I wanted U.C. Berkeley's law school on my resume.

What you can do to stand out.

If you're really serious about getting an LL.M degree, then one of the best things you can do is to differentiate yourself from the other students in the program. Use the LL.M and the entire experience as a test-drive for what you'd like to do later on in your professional career. Use it to publish articles, to connect with industry professionals, and to meet new professors and grow your network.

I've spoken to over one hundred LL.M students. The LL.M has opened some doors for them, but not many unless the school is highly regarded. A few of my mentees, for example, went to mid-level law schools for their LL.Ms (like George Washington University and Fordham) after they received a J.D. at a different, lower ranked law school. And the LL.M did not open many additional doors for them.

Getting an LL.M degree therefore has to be a strategic decision. If you're struggling to find a job as a lawyer with your J.D., getting an LL.M isn't going to necessarily turn the tides in your favor. In fact, it probably won't make a single bit of difference unless the LL.M itself pops out on your resume.

Pursuing education is never a bad decision—but it does require a strategy. If you see an end-goal in mind with your LL.M, then shoot for the stars. If not, figure out a different way to differentiate yourself.

CHAPTER 21:
How to Succeed as a Lawyer

Congratulations! You've made it to the end of this handbook—and with that, you should now have a wealth of knowledge, tips, and strategies to help you succeed in the process of getting hired as a lawyer. And guess what? Those skills are the very same skills that you'll need to succeed as a lawyer too.

Now, before I send you off into the real world, I have a few more tips up my sleeve that I want to leave you with.

Great lawyers are H.E.R.E.

H.E.R.E. is an acronym I like to use to remember the four essential traits of great lawyers.

Great lawyers are:
Honest;
Efficient;
Responsive; and
Effective.

They are honest about everything with their clients. They are efficient with their time. They are responsive to their clients. And they are effective at representing their clients.

Figure out which of those four are your weakest traits, and work on those. You need to excel at all of them to really nail it. If people know you're honest, efficient, responsive, and effective as an attorney, they'll always want to work with you.

Own your craft.

As a young associate, when I sent my work-product to a partner, it was absolutely the best I could produce. Always. No exceptions.

You have to always send your supervisor client-ready work, no matter how friendly you are with them. That way they won't have to work as much. And they can start building trust in you.

This is not negotiable.

You must take ownership of your writing, grammar, and professionalism. When you put your name on the dotted line, you're telling the world that this is your work. Yours.

Typos and grammar mistakes aren't a good look. Nor is being wrong.

To succeed as a lawyer and get hired as one, everything you say in writing and out loud must be correct, unless you expressly hedge your position. It's on you. Only you. No one else is going to take responsibility for your work.

Be terrified to screw up.

In your spam email. On your resume. In your cover letter. In your writing sample.

If you sign your name to something, make it your best. People will notice your attention to detail.

It sucks, but fear is part of being a lawyer. It's stressful and hard. But being scared to screw up is both normal and good.

If you want to be an amazing lawyer, you should want to do it the right way.

I still have nightmares about a project I did as a fourth-year associate where I missed a set of obscure federal Bureau of Land Management regulations. (Sorry again, Doug and Ann.) I literally just whiffed on the project.

I sent an email summarizing my research results and citing cases and the statute but not discussing or even citing the current federal regulations that answered the question. The partner then promptly reported my research results to the client.

It was the client who later (and rather nicely) pointed out our (really, *my*) mistake.

I was horrified.

The thing I've learned now as a partner, however, is that it's the associates who are scared to make mistakes who end up being the best lawyers.

<u>If you care that your work is correct, good things will happen to you.</u>

I cared a lot; maybe too much from a stress perspective. When I signed something as an associate (even an email), I always made sure it was my best work. Always. Then, if I screwed something up, I at least knew I had tried my best.

I think caring a lot is one of the primary reasons I have had success as a lawyer. You should care too; it's nice.

Treat supervisors like clients.

Remember that your client is not always whoever is paying for your work. Yes, that's where your legal and ethical obligations lie; but that's not what I'm talking about. I'm talking about your direct supervisor. You should view those people as if they're your clients too.

Is it self-serving for me to say that now as a partner at a law firm? Sure is. Will my current and future associates feel obligated to read my book, and then realize they should treat me like a client and be at my beck and call? Hopefully.

Still, the advice is sound.

You can have fun with your supervisors. Just treat them like bosses at work.

Your primary job is to make your direct supervisors look good. Do that, and you'll excel.

Have humility.

This is an important one because it's something that not enough lawyers and attorneys have these days. Being honest and humble about who you are, what you do, and why you do it will go a long way in your career. Having humility means that you hold yourself accountable, you're willing to listen to criticism, and you're prepared to do what it takes to become a better professional.

You don't know everything. You never have. You never will. But you can continue to build your wealth of knowledge and experience to make yourself the very best professional that you can be.

Say this to everyone you meet.

As a lawyer, you're going to meet quite a great deal of people throughout your career—and I hope that you treat them with the very same respect that you'd use for family and friends.

If you really want to succeed, try saying this to everyone you meet:

"My door is always open. If you ever want to meet with me, just send me an email."

Being available is one of the best qualities that you can offer someone—whether it be a colleague, a partner, or a client. Be open to having communications. Be open to listening. Be open to being a good person. Be open to honesty and transparency. And of course, be open to every single opportunity. One conversation can change your life, and one conversation with you can change someone else's life. Allow the world to unfold before you, and simply give things a chance to happen.

When you do that, nothing in this world will be able to stop you.

And don't forget, my door is always open too. If you have a question about what you've read in this book, if you'd like to comment on something that I've discussed, or if you'd like to share your story with me, I'd be happy to meet with you.

All you have to do is send me an email.

Your Get-a-Job Checklist

I know some people like lists, so here you go.

One-time Set Up Tasks:

- ☐ Calendar 30 to 60 minutes daily for your job search (Chapter 2)
- ☐ Google your name with and without quotes and see what comes up on the first four or five pages of results (Chapter 2)
- ☐ Professionalize your LinkedIn, Instagram, Twitter, Facebook, and any of your other public accounts (Chapter 2)
- ☐ Clean yourself up (Chapter 2)
- ☐ Figure out your rough value in the job market (Chapter 3)
- ☐ Learn how the business of law works (Chapters 4 & 17)
- ☐ Make a list of five geographies you're *willing* to live in (Chapter 5)
- ☐ Bookmark at least a few dozen online job pages you want to monitor (Chapter 12)
- ☐ Write three or four persuasive spam email templates asking for advice (Chapters 8 & 9)
- ☐ Edit your resume's education and experience sections using my tips (Chapter 10)
- ☐ Write an excellent cover letter (Chapter 11)
- ☐ Pick an interesting writing sample (Chapter 11)
- ☐ Write a cover page introduction for your writing sample (Chapter 11)
- ☐ Make sure your resume, cover letter, writing sample, and spam email templates comply with my five writing tips for dummies (Chapter 11)
- ☐ Get a few lawyers or law students to read and comment on your resume, cover letter, writing sample, and spam email templates, and then revise them accordingly (Chapter 9)

- ☐ Reach out to friends, family and your professional contacts to let them know about your job search (Chapter 7)
- ☐ Decide whether to specialize, and if so, in what area (Chapter 18)
- ☐ Connect with Brian H. Potts on LinkedIn (Chapter 7)

Daily Tasks:

- ☐ Don't get drunk with anyone who might hire you (Chapter 2)
- ☐ Check all your bookmarked online job pages
- ☐ Email and/or spam 20-30 lawyers asking for advice
- ☐ LinkedIn connect with 20-30 new lawyer contacts
- ☐ Get rejected and stay positive about it
- ☐ Act like you know what you're doing as a lawyer, even if you don't (Chapter 2)
- ☐ Don't do any of the things you shouldn't do when hunting for a job (Chapter 13)

Weekly Tasks:

- ☐ Zoom with two to three different, new professional acquaintances each week (Chapter 6)
- ☐ Get two new contacts from each of your Zoom meetings (Chapter 6)
- ☐ Go to at least one in-person social outing with a lawyer or business contact per week (Chapter 6)
- ☐ Spend an hour doing something nice for at least two of your professional contacts per week (Chapter 7)
- ☐ Email and/or spam as many people as you need to each week to ensure your networking goals are met (Chapter 7)
- ☐ Find and apply to as many job postings online as you can (Chapter 12)
- ☐ Prepare for all your interviews using my tips (Chapter 14)
- ☐ Get a job
- ☐ Tell all your friends about this book

My Guarantee to You

I believe in the methods I've written about in this book. And I sincerely hope it helps you. If it does, and you get a job, please tell a friend about it.

But if you are employable as a lawyer, and you don't get a job within a reasonable amount of time after reading this book—or if you just want to lie to me and get a refund—all you have to do is email me (**brianhpotts@gmail.com**) with your story. I'll happily refund your money and wish you the best of luck in your continued search.

—Brian H. Potts

Printed in the USA
CPSIA information can be obtained
at www.ICGtesting.com
LVHW092047030124
767895LV00014B/726

9 781955 342209